DATE DUE			
JUN 76	JUN 92		
JUN 72	JUN 9		
OCT 17			
MAY 28			
JUN 78			
JUN 79			
JUN 80			
JUN 81			
JUN 82			
JUN 83			
JUN 84			
JUN 85			
APR 20			
MAY 10			
JUN 86			
JUN 87			
JUN 88			
JUN 89			
JUN 91			

IDEAL 3370 UNGUMMED, 3371 GUMMED

KEEPING
THE PLANTS
YOU PICK

KEEPING THE PLANTS YOU PICK

LAURA LOUISE FOSTER

ILLUSTRATED BY THE AUTHOR

THOMAS Y. CROWELL COMPANY
NEW YORK

Designed by Elke Schwarz Sigal

Manufactured in the United States of America
L.C. Card 74–101926
ISBN 0-690-47140-8
4   5   6   7   8   9   10
Published in Canada by Fitzhenry & Whiteside Limited, Toronto.

To my mother, Louise R. James,
whose exquisite flower arrangements
are my inspiration and my despair

CONTENTS

KEEPING
THE PLANTS
YOU PICK

1
YOU CAN
PRESERVE
PLANTS

How pleasant it is to gather a few flowers as you wander through grassy meadows or in deep cool woods where specks of sunlight sift through the leaves and spangle the carpet of ferns. What fun it is to walk along a country road or garden path choosing blossoms, leaves, and grasses for the vase in your bedroom or for an arrangement in the living room. And how lovely are the flowers you picked, lighting a dark corner in the hall or creating a splash of color on the dinner table—but how briefly they last.

In a week, sometimes in as short a time as a few days they begin to droop. The petals curl and become streaked with brown. Soon your lovely bouquet is limp and sad and fit only for the scrap basket. How nice it would be if you could enjoy the flowers you pick a little longer.

It is possible to preserve flowers so that they *will* last for months or even longer. Preserved plants can be used for flower arrangements and for making many other pretty things.

Plants can be preserved in many ways. Most of them can be dried by pressing but many can be dried without being pressed. Some plants will keep their shape if they are put in a warm airy place so that the air will dry them. Others must be buried in special materials called desiccants, which absorb all their moisture but keep them from shriveling. Some leaves can be preserved by being put in a special fluid, which they will suck up. This prevents them from becoming brittle. In this book you will find descriptions of these different methods of preservation and suggestions about the best kinds of plants to preserve by each method. There are also chapters about the things you can make with pressed plants and the ways you can arrange preserved plants in containers to decorate the rooms in your house.

Many of the plants mentioned in this book can be found in woods and fields, and along the sides of country roads. Some grow in flower and vegetable gardens. A few cannot be found in the wild and are seldom grown in gardens. They have been included, however, because they preserve extremely easily and are not difficult to grow. You might want to try growing some of these special flowers in your own garden.

Strawflower

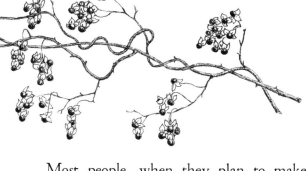

2
GATHERING PLANTS

Most people, when they plan to make a flower arrangement, think only of flowers. But there are many other parts of a plant besides the flowers that are decorative. Many plants have handsome leaves, and in autumn some of these are as brightly colored as any flower. The fruits of some plants are also very beautiful. When you are selecting plants for dried flower arrangements, consider including attractive leaves and fruits as well as flowers.

The fruits of different plants vary in color, size, shape, and texture. Every flower eventually becomes a fruit that contains the seed of the plant. Making seeds is the real function of a flower. Without seeds there would be no new plants to take the place of those that die. Some fruits, such as peaches and strawberries, are fleshy and edible.

4

Strawberry

Gathering Plants

Most fleshy fruits rot or shrivel and cannot be preserved. But not all fruits are fleshy and soft when they are ripe. Nuts and some berries, such as those of holly and climbing bittersweet, are hard and dry when they are ripe and will not decay after they are picked. These can be attractive additions to dried flower arrangements.

Some fruits, such as string beans, are pods or seed capsules. When bean pods are ripe they become stiff and brittle and the seeds inside are hard as pebbles. Pea plants, okra, lilies, irises, and many other plants have their seeds inside pods. Short fat seed pods, such as those of poppies, are frequently called seed capsules.

Many seed capsules and seed pods that contain hard, heavy seeds burst open when they are ripe and shoot their seeds long distances. These fruits usually shatter as they burst and for that reason do not dry well. Other seed pods contain lightweight or flaky seeds that are readily blown about by the wind. These pods open more gradually and are likely to retain their shape as they dry.

Some plants do not keep their seeds in pods, capsules, or fleshy fruits but carry them in clusters called seed heads. Some seed heads are made up of bunches of many small pods or capsules; but some plants, such as grasses, rushes, and the various weeds known as dock, have seed heads

5

Acorn

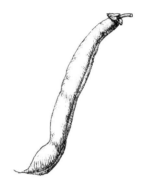

Stringbean

Close-up of seed covering

Seed head of orchard grass

Seeds of
curly dock

Curly dock

that are made up of many individual seeds, each one wrapped in a scalelike covering that is separately fastened to the stem of the plant. This kind of seed head usually dries well. Some other plants, such as dandelions, daisies, buttercups, and goldenrod, carry seed heads made up of many separate seeds that are attached to a pad or fleshy stalk. These seed heads are likely to go to pieces if they are picked after the seeds have formed.

The fruits, flowers, and leaves of some plants are very colorful. Others are interesting chiefly because of their shapes and textures. When you see a plant at a distance, it is the color that catches your eye. But when you look closely, the shape and texture is often as important. Arrangements of plant material used to decorate a room are usually seen at close range. Shape and texture are particularly significant when you are picking leaves, flowers, and fruits you plan to preserve, because frequently their colors fade somewhat in the process.

Part of the fun of gathering plants for arrangements is finding them unexpectedly along the roadside, or in the woods and fields. Keep your eyes open when you are out walking. Usually no one minds if you pick plants along the edge of a country road. But remember that the fields and woods are someone's property. It is always

Dandelion seed head

best to ask permission at a nearby house before you gather flowers. Most people will not mind your picking some flowers if you ask first.

The flowers in public parks and gardens should not be picked. They are grown to be looked at. If everyone picked a few, there would soon be none left to see. And, of course, you should never pick flowers in any private garden, except your very own, without asking permission.

Most of the plants that grow along country roadsides and in the fields are quite common. Many of those that preserve most easily are weeds, such as cow vetch and buttercups. It will do no harm if you gather a few of these. But some wild flowers are rare and should be picked cautiously or, in some cases, not at all.

If you see only a few specimens of a plant, this may mean that it is rare, and you will be wise to pick no more than one or two. You should never pick a wild flower if it is the only one of its kind. It should be left to grow and make seeds. In fact you should always leave some of every

7

Cow vetch

kind of wild flower, no matter how many there are, so that they can turn into seeds from which new plants can grow.

A plant will not be harmed if its flowers are picked carefully. It is always best to cut stems or branches with a pair of scissors or clippers. Many plants have tough stems, and you can injure a plant or even tear it up by the roots if you try to break the stalk with your fingers. A stem cut sharply and neatly heals quickly. A ragged, broken stem does not heal easily, and disease may get in and kill the plant.

Also, if you cut the stem instead of trying to break it, you are more likely to get the length you want. No matter how you plan to preserve the plant you should cut it with a fairly long stem. You can always shorten the stem later if you find it is too long for your purpose.

But never cut all the leaves off a standing plant. A plant must have leaves in order to feed itself. All the nourishment a plant needs to live and grow is made by the leaves. The water a plant sucks up through its roots contains many chemicals. The plant cannot use these until they have been changed into a food it can digest. The leaves are the food factories that change the chemicals into plant food. Without foliage a plant would starve and die.

8

Gathering Plants

If you do not disturb the roots and if you leave at least half the leaves on the standing plant, it will eventually grow a new set of flowers, and these will become seeds from which new plants can develop. Gather your flowers carefully and do not be greedy, so that you do not destroy the plants from which you pick.

Common buttercup

3
PLANT COLLECTIONS

There are several different ways of preserving the plants you gather. The easiest method is to dry them by pressing them between sheets of absorbent paper. Plants that have been pressed and dried can be used to make pictures, bookmarks, place mats, and greeting cards. This is also the method to use if you want to make a collection of the plants that grow near your home.

Botanists, the scientists who study plants, make collections of pressed, dried plants. Dried plants are very brittle, however, and they will get broken if they are handled very much or kept loose in a drawer or box. To protect the pressed plants in their collections, botanists fasten them to big sheets of lightweight cardboard and keep these in folders. Such a collection of pressed plants

10

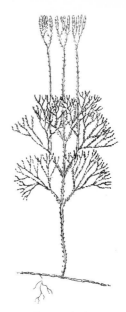

is called a herbarium. Plants that have been properly pressed and mounted on cardboard can last for many years. Some herbariums in museums and universities are three hundred years old and are still in good condition.

The sheets of thin cardboard on which the plants are mounted are called herbarium sheets. Each sheet is carefully labeled with the name of the plant and the place and date it was found. The herbarium sheets are then arranged in groups according to how closely the plants on them are related to each other. For instance, all the herbarium sheets of ferns will be kept in one folder. All the herbarium sheets of ground pine will be kept in another folder. These two folders will be kept next to each other because ferns and ground pines are very closely related. By arranging their herbarium sheets in family groups, botanists can quickly find any particular plant they may be looking for.

Ground pine

Scientific herbariums are used for a number of purposes. By studying the plants in herbariums it is possible to find out what plants grow in different parts of the world. The authors of books that describe wild flowers found in a certain area check through herbariums to make sure they have mentioned all the plants that grow in the area they are writing about. The artists who illustrate wild-flower

11

Broad beech fern

books often use the dried flowers in herbariums as models.

Herbariums are also used to identify plants. If a botanist discovers a plant he does not recognize, he compares it to similar specimens in the herbarium. In many cases he is able to identify it exactly. If by chance his plant has never been found before, he can determine what group it belongs to, give the new plant a name, and put a pressed specimen in the correct folder in the herbarium.

You can make a herbarium of the wild flowers you find in your neighborhood or a collection of leaves from all the trees that grow in your area.

Instead of dividing your plants into family groups you might arrange them according to where they grow. You could put swamp plants in one folder and the flowers you find in the woods in another folder. Or you could arrange your plants according to the season of the year in which they bloom, starting with hepaticas and spring beauties and ending with goldenrod and asters.

You need to pick only one flower stalk of each kind for a herbarium. Cut the stem quite long, since you should have some of the stem and some of the leaves, as well as the flower, to fasten to your herbarium sheet. Certain plants, such as hepaticas and some violets, do not have leaves on the flower stalk but on separate stalks coming

Hepatica flower and leaf

up from the root. When you collect a specimen of this kind, be sure to collect a leaf as well as a flower stalk.

When you bring home plants you are planning to press, you should put them in water unless you are going to do the job right away or unless they are so wilted that the petals are crumpled and the leaves beginning to curl. It is easier, however, to arrange plants for pressing if they are slightly wilted.

PRESSING PLANTS

Botanists use special plant presses that are light and easy to carry. These are convenient if you are exploring for plants in a jungle or camping for weeks at a time in the mountains. You can buy such a plant press in a scientific supply store if you think you will need one. But all you

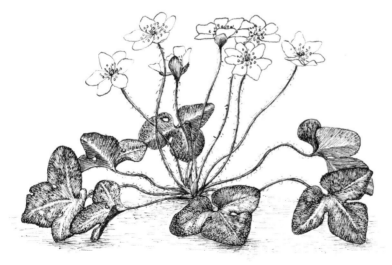

Round-lobed hepatica

really need at home are some sheets of newspaper and a few heavy books.

The newspaper is used to make folded pads to absorb the moisture from the plants. These folded pads of paper are called driers. Use regular newspaper to make your driers. The shiny kind of paper that is sometimes used for the magazine section is not absorbent enough. It is also better not to use the colored comic pages because the colors of the pictures might stain the flowers. If you

Strap

Folded newspaper or blotters

Heavy books

Wooden lattice covers

Folded newspaper

Professional plant press

Homemade plant press

are very fussy, you can put a paper towel on the sheet of newspaper before you put your plant on it. Then place another paper towel on top of the plant before you fold the top layer of newspaper over it. This will keep the black ink of the print from rubbing off on the leaves and petals. Usually it will not come off very much anyway unless the newspaper is a very recent one.

Make your driers by placing two big unfolded sheets of newspaper on top of each other. Fold these in half along the crease that is already there. Then fold the sheets in half again. Your folded drier should now be about seventeen inches long and eleven inches wide. When you have pressed the creases well with your hand, open the folded paper again so that it is the size it was before you folded it the second time. You will now have four layers of paper with a crease down the middle. If you are using the small, tabloid-size newspaper, use four sheets laid out flat one on top of the other.

Arrange your plant carefully on one side of this drier. Do not let any of the leaves or stems project over the crease onto the other half of the paper. If your plant is very big you may have to cut off some of the bottom of the stem to make it fit on the sheet.

If all the leaves on the stem are on this bottom end, cut the stem a few inches below the flower and again a little above the leafy part. Press these two ends for your herbarium sheet and throw away the middle part of the stem. Sometimes a plant, such as a fern, has a very big leaf that will not fit on the drier. You can cut such a leaf in several pieces and press these pieces in several driers. Or you can fold the leaf or plant, instead of cutting it, so that it all fits on one drier. Fold the stem on a slant so that one half does not lie directly on top of the other half.

Try to arrange your plant on the drier so that the flower petals and leaves are not crumpled. If you have to fold a stem or leaf, do it neatly. Spread out and separate the leaves as much as possible so that they are not bunched on top of each other. It sometimes helps to smooth them carefully with your fingers and even press down on them gently with your hand. You may find it easier to arrange a troublesome plant if you let it lie flat on the newspaper for a while so it can wilt a little and get limp. The stem, leaves, and petals are more likely to stay in position if they are not too stiff.

Do not try to crowd too many plants onto one drying pad. If you place several plants on the same drier keep them well separated so the leaves and flowers do not overlap. Plants can stick together as they dry, and it is hard to get them apart without tearing them. Also, the color of one plant might stain another. In addition, the faster your plants dry the more natural their color will be, and a bunch of leaves or petals will not dry quickly. If you have many plants to dry at one time, make several drying pads with plants inside each one. It is important to arrange your plants carefully on the driers because once they are pressed and dried you will not be able to change their shape.

When the plants have been arranged on one side of the crease in the drying pad, carefully fold the other half of the drier over them.

Once all the plants you want to press are inside folded

driers, they are ready for pressing. You should put the driers in a warm, dry place while the plants are being pressed. They should be kept out of the way because it will take at least a week for the plants to dry thoroughly. You might put them on the floor in a corner or under a table. Leaves and small, delicate blossoms will usually be pressed dry in a week. Thick flowers, such as roses, may take two weeks or even longer to dry.

You can pile the driers one on top of the other while they are being pressed. Handle them carefully while you are moving them and piling them up. Keep them as flat as possible when you lift them and do not tip them, or the plants inside may get rumpled or even fall out from between the sheets of newspaper. Pile the driers neatly so their edges meet.

Then put a layer of heavy books on top of the pile. Their weight will press the plants and keep the leaves and petals from shriveling as they dry.

It does no harm to examine your plants from time to time to see how they are drying. Be very careful when you unpile the driers. Open them cautiously because sometimes the plants stick to the sheet on top of them. If this happens, pull them loose very gently and lay them flat on the bottom sheet before closing the drier.

You can use the same newspaper driers over and over again.

If you want to wait for a rainy day or until winter to fasten your plants to herbarium sheets, you can leave them in the driers. Put a piece of paper in the drier with each plant, telling what it is and where you found it. It is very easy to forget these facts, and you will want to remember them when it comes time to label the herbarium sheets.

MOUNTING PLANTS

You will need big pieces of heavy paper for your herbarium sheets. Oak tag or other thin cardboard is excellent for this purpose. Your plants will show up best on white or cream-colored paper.

All your herbarium sheets should be the same size. Also, it is usually most convenient if they are the same size as your folded driers, so that they will hold the largest plants you have pressed. You can always put more than one specimen on a sheet if your plants are small. Of course if all your plants are little you can use smaller herbarium sheets.

You may use separate sheets and keep your collection

of pressed plants in a flat box. Or, if you prefer, you can fasten your leaves and flowers onto the pages of a large photograph album. Use one with white or cream-colored rather than black pages. Whether you use loose sheets or the pages of an album, fasten your dried plants on only one side.

The plants should be thoroughly dry and quite stiff before you fasten them to your herbarium sheets. If they are still moist and limp they may shrivel and curl when they are no longer weighted down in the driers.

Since you will probably not want to take the plants off the herbarium sheets once they are fastened down, you can glue them directly to the sheets. Use a glue that will not stain the plants or the sheets. The kind of liquid glue that is white and creamy when you put it on but becomes clear and colorless when it is dry is good to use. The white of raw egg is also an excellent glue for fastening down plants, particularly if they are small and delicate. Egg-white glue is completely transparent when it is dry and will not stain the thinnest petals.

To make egg-white glue, separate the white part of the egg from the yolk. It takes a little practice to do this without breaking the yolk. A few drops of yellow mixed with the white will do no great harm, but try to keep as

where it is to go. Press down on one end first. Smooth the strip across the plant so that it fits tightly before you press down on the other end. The gluey ends of the paper strip should come as close as possible to the plant without touching it. Either white library paste or white glue is fine for this job. Do not put too much glue on the ends of your fastener or it will squish out and get on the plant when you press down on the ends. A toothpick or small, stiff brush are good tools for putting the right amount of glue on the ends of the paper fastener.

Put paper strips across your plant in several places so that it cannot slip around. You should put at least two fasteners across the main stalk. One of these should go right under the flowers. The other should go near the bottom end of the stalk. If your stem is long, you may want to put another strip across the middle.

You should also put strips across any branches that stick out on either side of the main stem. If the leaves are large you may need to put fasteners across their stalks so that they will not get broken off. Do not put strips across the leaves or flowers themselves if you can help it. But if a leaf is very large you may have to put a fastener across the tip to hold it securely. If you are making a collection of single leaves, fasten them down with strips

25

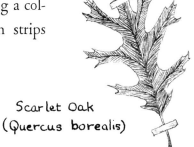

Scarlet Oak
(Quercus borealis)

across the stalk and the tip, rather than across the middle.

Once your plant material is either glued down or fastened down with paper strips, let the herbarium sheet dry thoroughly before labeling it. The labels can be written directly on the sheet or on a separate piece of paper that you glue in place.

First write down the name of the plant. If you do not know the name ask someone who does. Or look it up in a book about the wild flowers that grow in your area. Public libraries usually have several books of this kind that you can borrow. In the back of this book there is a list of some books about wild flowers that you may find useful.

Underneath the name of the plant write the date you picked it and where you found it. Page 27 shows an example of a labeled herbarium sheet.

You will notice that there are two names written under the plant on the herbarium sheet. The first name, columbine, is this plant's common name in English. The name in parentheses, *Aquilegia canadensis*, is the scientific, botanical name.

You do not have to write the botanical name on your herbarium sheet unless you want to. But botanists always use botanical names when they write or talk about plants.

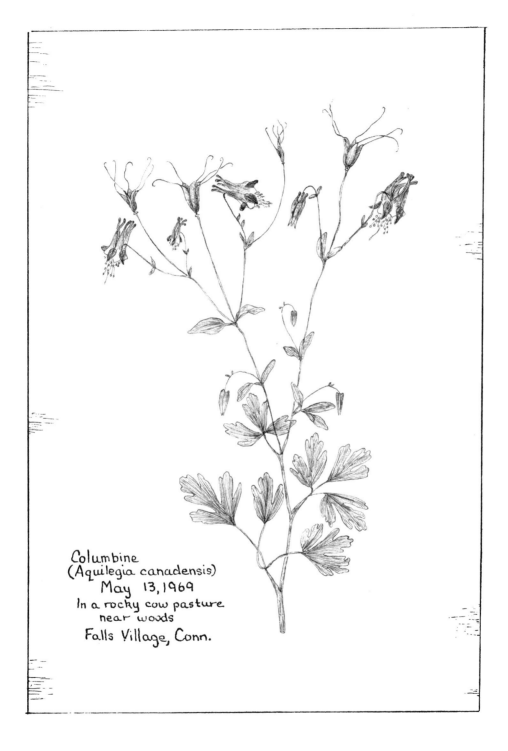

Columbine
(Aquilegia canadensis)
May 13, 1969
In a rocky cow pasture
near woods
Falls Village, Conn.

Plant Collections

Common names of plants can be very confusing. Most plants have more than one common name. Also many different plants may all have the same common name.

The plant pictured on the herbarium sheet is called columbine in most parts of England and America. But in France its common name is "ancolie." A German would call it "akelei." In some parts of the United States this plant is called honeysuckle, which is also the common name of several different kinds of bushes and vines.

The common name of a plant is a little like a person's nickname. You and your friends know who you mean when you use each other's nicknames, but you could not use a nickname to look up somebody's telephone number.

For many years even botanists called plants only by their common names. But as there got to be more and more botanists and gardeners in different parts of the world they soon discovered that it was impossible to talk about a particular plant if it had several different names.

Finally, in 1735, a Swedish botanist called Linnaeus worked out a system that all scientists agreed to use. In this system every kind of plant was given a two-part Latin name. Linnaeus chose Latin for these botanical names because this was the international language every scientist

28

Aquilegia alpina *Aquilegia coerulea*

Two kinds of columbine flowers

and every educated man could understand, no matter what country he came from.

The first part of a plant's botanical name is rather like your family name. All plants in the same closely related group, or genus, have similar blossoms and seed capsules and are given the same first name. All columbines, no matter where they come from, have similar blossoms and seed capsules and have the same first name: *Aquilegia.*

But all the plants in the genus called *Aquilegia* are not exactly alike. Some have petals with short stubby tubes that stick up out of the top of their flowers. Some have petals with very long slender tubes, or spurs, as they usually are called. In the western part of the United States there are columbines with blue and white blossoms, with yellow blossoms, and with red blossoms. The columbine pictured on the herbarium sheet grows in northeastern America and has red and yellow flowers.

Some of these differently colored columbines have

29

Seed pod of columbine

long tubes; others are short-tubed. Some are plants only two inches tall; others grow several feet high. In Japan, China, and Europe there are still other columbines of various heights and with flowers of somewhat different shapes and color combinations.

Aquilegia is not the only genus made up of several kinds of plants that look different, even though their seed pods and flowers resemble each other closely. Almost every genus contains plants with a few important characteristics that make them look somewhat different from their relatives.

For this reason Linnaeus divided every genus into even smaller groups, which he called species. Every plant belonging to the same species has its own special species name. This name is placed after the plant's genus name, and the two names together are its botanical name.

In this way every known kind of plant has received its own botanical name. This means that botanists and other people interested in plants can be sure, if they use this name, that they are all talking about the same particular kind of plant. This prevents a great many mistakes. A gardener can order a particular kind of plant from a nursery, even a foreign nursery, and be fairly sure he will get what he wants. This also means that a French botanist, or a German botanist, or an American botanist can look up plants in a herbarium made by a Russian botanist, even though none of them can speak or read Russian.

You can add plants to the collection in your herbarium every year. If you go on a summer vacation you can make a special herbarium of the plants you collect on your trip.

Meadowsweet

4
PRESSED
FLOWER
PICTURES

There are many ways of using pressed plants other than putting them into herbariums. They also make delightful pictures, which can be framed and hung on the wall. Pictures made of pressed flowers, leaves, and grasses can also be used to make very pretty greeting cards, bookmarks, and other things you can give away as presents or use yourself.

MATERIALS

You can use most kinds of flowers, leaves, and grasses for making flower pictures as long as they can be pressed really flat.

The color of a flower frequently changes when it is

dry. But the color itself is not an indication of whether it will change or not. For example, some kinds of yellow flowers stay yellow when they are dry. Other yellow flowers may turn orange or even brown. You will have to experiment with the various blossoms you pick to discover which ones dry to a pleasant color.

Flowers that have a hard, thickened lump just below the petals are difficult to press. This lump is called the receptacle, and it holds the baby seeds. It will eventually ripen into a fruit. Roses and apple blossoms are examples of flowers that protect their seeds inside this kind of receptacle.

Blossoms that have a great many layers of overlapping petals, such as double peonies and zinnias, are also difficult to press really flat. In addition, they tend to look rather shapeless when they are pressed.

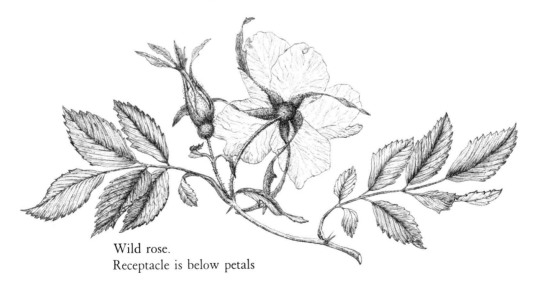

Wild rose.
Receptacle is below petals

Pressed Flower Pictures

It is possible, however, to make pictures with flowers that have thick receptacles or many layers of petals. Snip off the petals and dry them individually. You can use these in your pictures either separately or in groups.

The beauty of a well-designed flower picture results from the delicate lines of the stems and from the shapes of dainty flowers and feathery leaves silhouetted against the background. Flowers with only a few petals or with only a single layer of separated petals look well in flower pictures. Small leaves, with interesting shapes, are the best kinds to put in a picture. Lacy and ferny leaves and medium-sized leaves with notches and points around the edges are better than large leaves that are smooth and even in outline. The delicate stems and feathery flower heads of grasses are wonderfully graceful when pressed.

Choose little flowers and small, ferny leaves and grasses, and even single flower petals for small pictures. Many wild flowers have small flowers that are particularly suitable for this kind of picture. Sprigs of really tiny flowers, such as those of the tall-stemmed flower called yellow sweet clover, are very useful. You can also use individual flowers of plants such as larkspur and hydrangea, which carry their blossoms in sprays, spikes, and bunches. It is best to snip off the individual flowers before you press them.

Individual hydrangea flowers

34

Yellow sweet clover

Larkspur

Individual flower cluster

Queen Anne's lace

Other types of blossoms, such as Queen Anne's lace and steeplebush, are made up of many small clusters of tiny flowers. These blossoms can be snipped apart into several clusters before they are dried. Each separate little cluster is a good size for use in small pictures.

There are also many garden plants that are excellent for making flower pictures. If you keep your eyes open as you walk in the garden, or in the fields, you will find many little flowers that are suitable. Be sure to collect a number of feathery grasses and delicate ferny leaves too.

You can collect larger flowers and leaves for making big pictures. Ferns and some of the sturdy grasses and rushes are fine for this purpose. And, of course, autumn leaves, with or without added flowers, can be used to make wonderfully gay, colorful pictures.

36

Pressed Flower Pictures

For a herbarium you only need to collect one specimen of each kind of plant, but for flower pictures you should pick quite a number of each kind. Several flowers and leaves of the same general shape and color scattered throughout your design will usually make a more attractive picture than a design made of many different kinds of flowers.

It is a good idea to dry a large number of flowers, leaves, and grasses so that you will have a wide choice of material to work with. You can start collecting and pressing flowers in the spring and keep collecting suitable plant material all summer.

Press and dry your plants for pictures in the way described in the previous chapter for pressing plants for your herbarium.

When your plants have been properly pressed and dried, you can take them out from between the drying sheets and store them in covered cardboard boxes until you are ready to use them. Handle them carefully. Pressed, dried plants are fragile and break easily. You can lay them one on top of the other, but be sure they are flat. Do not fill your box too full or the plants will be crushed when you put the lid on. If you put two or three chunks of raw apple or raw potato, wrapped in a paper towel, in the corner of the box it will help keep the dried plants from becoming too brittle.

If you prefer, you can leave the plants between the drying sheets until you are ready to use them. But putting them in boxes takes up less room and allows you to use the drying sheets for other plants.

It is a good idea to keep different types of material in separate boxes: flowers in one box, grasses in another, small ferny leaves separate from larger leaves. In this way you can find more quickly the type of material you want when you start designing your picture.

You will need a big table covered with newspaper when you start making your flower pictures, since you will need plenty of room to work and spread out all your materials.

It is a good idea to make your first picture rather small and simple. This will give you practice in arranging and gluing down the plants. Later on you can make more complicated pictures. For your first picture you might make one to hang on the wall in your room or to give to your mother as a present.

Pictures that are going to be hung on the wall are best framed behind glass or covered with some other kind of transparent material to protect the flowers so that they will not become dusty or broken.

38

Pressed Flower Pictures

Pictures that will be framed behind glass can be made on heavy white drawing paper or very thin white cardboard. Buy the frame first and make your picture the right size to fit. Directions for doing this can be found in the next chapter. But picture frames cost money. It might be better to cover your first picture with the kind of transparent plastic film used for wrapping food. Your mother probably has a roll of this film in the kitchen. This method of protecting flower pictures is also described in the next chapter.

If you are going to cover your picture with thin plastic film you will have to glue the plants onto a piece of cardboard that is quite stiff. It should be white. The slender leaves and stems of dried plants will not show up well from a distance against a dark or colored background. Fairly strong, flat gift boxes—the kind made to hold dresses, shirts, and sweaters—are usually made of cardboard that is about the right stiffness. The insides of the lids of these boxes are usually white and not too shiny.

For your first picture cut out a white cardboard rectangle about eight inches long and six inches wide, or a little larger. Use a ruler to measure the lines and get them straight. The corner of a book, magazine, or pad of paper will help you get the lines at right angles to each

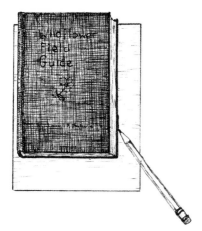

other in the corners. When you have drawn your outline, cut around it with a pair of strong, sharp scissors.

In addition to this piece of cardboard you will need glue. You should glue your plants directly to the background, just as you do for herbarium sheets. The kinds of glue to use and the implements and methods for using them have been described in the previous chapter.

You will also need a pair of small, sharp, pointed scissors for snipping off stems and leaves. If you are planning to use very small, delicate pieces of plant material, you may need a pair of tweezers to hold them while you put glue on their backs and place them in the correct position on the background. It is also wise to have some clean toothpicks and some small, clean rags and a basin of water nearby, in case you need to mop up glue that has dripped in the wrong place.

In addition to these implements, put your boxes of dried, pressed plants on the table so they are easy to reach.

DESIGNING AND MAKING A PICTURE

You should always lay out the plan of your picture before you start to work with glue. Flower pictures are made up of two or more layers of plant material. It will be easier to make a pleasing design if you decide where the flowers, stems, and leaves look best before you start gluing them into place. Once they are glued down you will not be able to move them.

A simple spray of a few mixed flowers, leaves, and grasses is a good design to start with. A spray is a loose bunch of plants with the lower parts of some of the stems showing below the leaves and flowers.

Start planning your design by placing on your cardboard background the plants you want in the bottom layer. Your finished picture will look better if you leave a margin of blank background around the design. Place your first layer of plants with this in mind. First place a few fine grasses and thin stems of small leaves and flowers in a semicircle as an outline around the top and sides of your finished bunch of flowers. It is best to use rather short-stemmed grasses and short sprigs of leafy and flowering stems for this bottom layer. The bottom ends of these stems should point in toward the center of your design but should not cross each other. You will be putting another layer of leaves and flowers over the ends of their stems. Only their tops will show around the top and sides of the finished spray.

41

Let a few areas of the background paper show between these sprigs in the bottom layer. The flowers and leaves in the second layer will slightly overlap the plants in the layer beneath and help fill the blank spaces. It is always better not to have too many layers of plants glued directly on top of each other, or eventually you will end up with a thick wad of plants that will not lie flat and firm on the background. Use a sharp pair of scissors to snip off stems that are too long and any leaves that will be hidden by the plants on top.

Once you have arranged the plants in the bottom layer, lay the next layer of leaves and flowers. Their upper ends should fill in some of the blank spaces between the plants already arranged and they should cover most of the stem ends. You will probably find that you need to further shorten some of the stems in your bottom layer and trim off a leaf or two.

Leave some of the stems in the second layer long enough to show at the bottom of the finished spray. Five long stems showing below the leaves and flowers are usually enough. Snip off the other stems so that they end part-way up in the spray.

Add a third layer of a few leaves and flowers to cover the stem ends that are still showing in the middle of the spray. This last top layer of leaves and flowers should have no stems at all. You can also scatter two or three stemless flowers or single petals on top of the plants already in place to fill blank spaces, add a bit of color in a spot that needs it, or cover an ugly leaf.

Bottom layer

Second layer added

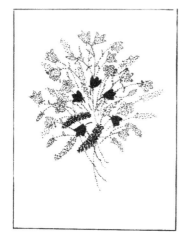

Third layer added

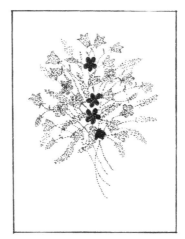

Finishing touches added

As you arrange the layers of plants, you will see that the beauty of a well-designed flower picture results from the delicate lines of the stems and the shapes of the flowers and leaves silhouetted against the background. It is best if you do not make the mass of plants too dense.

When you have placed your plant material in a design that pleases you, take it off the background one layer at a time. Lay each layer separately on the table, placing the plants in about the same position they will be in when they are glued to the finished picture. This will help you to remember where they go when you glue them down for good. The plants in the bottom layer can be left in place on the background sheet. You can pick these up one at a time to put glue on the back and then immediately replace them in position.

Glue down each layer of plants in the way described for gluing plants to herbarium sheets. Use as little glue as possible. Egg-white glue is probably best to fasten down very small, delicate plants. You can coat the whole back with a watercolor brush without danger of staining the petals.

Allow the glue on the first layer of plants to harden for a few minutes until it is no longer sticky before you put more plants on top. Try out the positions of the stems, leaves, and flowers in your second layer before you put any glue on them. It is always safest to test the position of each bit of plant material you plan to add to your picture before you glue it down. It is almost impossible to change the position of a gluey stem or leaf without tearing it or messing up the picture.

When all the plants are firmly fastened in place, allow the picture to dry for two or three hours before handling it further. Then you will be able to cover it with transparent plastic film. You will find directions for doing this in the next chapter.

OTHER DESIGNS FOR PICTURES

After you have made one or two simple pictures you will probably want to try making more complicated ones.

The kind of paper you use for the background and the size to which you cut it depend on the protective covering you plan to put over the picture. You can use heavy drawing paper or very thin cardboard if your picture is going to be framed behind glass. You should always cut the paper to fit the frame before planning your design. If you want to protect your picture by spraying it with liquid plastic or by covering it with a sheet of transparent

45

plastic, you should make the picture on stiff cardboard. The lids of cardboard boxes are stiff enough for small pictures, but really heavy cardboard is needed for pictures larger than eight inches square. In art-supply stores and in some stationery and department stores you can buy big sheets of stiff illustration board or mounting board with a white surface especially made as a background for pictures. These come in several different thicknesses. The bigger your picture, the thicker your cardboard should be.

You can make your own illustration board or mounting board by pasting a sheet of drawing paper onto a piece of heavy cardboard. But it is not easy to do this well. You must be sure to spread the paste or glue evenly over the entire back of the paper so that it will stick to the cardboard smoothly and tightly, with no wrinkles or air bubbles underneath. Keep the cardboard pressed flat under heavy books until the glue is thoroughly dry. Then paste another piece of paper onto the back of the cardboard. This can be ordinary wrapping paper. Unless you paste paper onto both sides of the cardboard, it will curl even after it is dry.

Once you have decided what kind of background paper you should use, you can arrange stems, leaves, and flowers on it in a number of different ways.

Pressed Flower Pictures

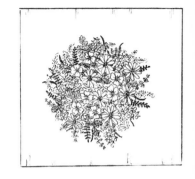

Bouquets are always attractive. These are made layer by layer in the same way you make a spray except that *all* the stem ends are hidden under flowers and leaves glued over them. Try making bouquets of different shapes. You can make them round or triangular or oval. To keep the stems from showing, they should be kept short in every layer of the bouquet. Place the plants on the edges of your design first and work toward the middle, so that the last layer of flowers and leaves covers all the stem ends. You may find you will need more than three layers of plants for bouquets, particularly if your picture is a big one. But even large pictures will be more attractive if you do not place the plants too thickly on the background. Let some of the paper show between the plants in all your pictures.

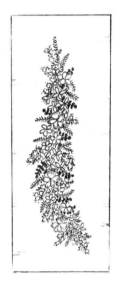

You might also try arranging your flowers in the shape of a wreath or garland. A wreath can be square, oval, round, triangular, or even heart-shaped. A garland can be straight or wavy. It will be easier to make this kind of design if you first outline the desired shape very lightly with pencil on the background. Then place the first layer of plants so they stick out a little way on either side of the penciled line. The next layers of plants will be placed inside this first layer so as to cover the stem ends. Two

47

or at the most three layers of plants will probably be enough. The stems of the plants in all the layers should be very short.

You can use more than a single group of flowers for a design. You can make a wreath as a frame around a small bouquet; you can place a large bouquet or wreath on one part of the background and put one or two small sprays of flowers on another part. You can scatter a few single sprigs of very small flowers in the space around the main spray or bouquet. Or you can place a scattering of single, stemless flowers or separate petals in the margin around the main group of plant material.

You can cover the whole background of a fairly large picture with a solid patchwork of overlapping green leaves or brightly colored autumn leaves. Scatter over this leafy background a few groups of stemless flowers of a contrasting color. Pale lavender asters or white daisies show up well against a background of dark red and maroon leaves. Deep purple asters or single blossoms from a spike of monkshood or delphinium look well against orange and yellow leaves. Or you can scatter daisies, buttercups, and small orange and red poppies on a background of green leaves.

You can also arrange your flowers to make them look

48

Bird's-foot violet

as if they were growing. One way to do this is to place a group of leaves and flowers in the shape of a fan with the ends of all the stalks placed close together at the bottom. Cover this bunch of stem ends with a few stemless leaves. Such an arrangement will look more natural if all the flowers and all the leaves you use are of the same kind. The stemless leaves that cover the stem ends could be either the same or a different kind. You could use brown autumn leaves to cover the stem ends of early spring flowers, such as crocuses, scillas, Dutchman's-breeches, or hepaticas. These would then look as if they were growing out of the ground cover of dead leaves in the woods.

49

You can also make plants look as if they were growing by placing a mixture of flower stalks and grasses in a row about two layers thick. Cover the stem ends at the bottom of the row with small green leaves. Or, if you plan to put your picture in a frame that has a mat which fits between the picture and the glass, you can use the mat to cover the stem ends. A mat is a piece of cardboard that is cut out in the center. Before you make your picture place the mat on top of the background paper and trace the outline of the opening in the mat onto it. Then place the row of flowers and grass stems so that the ends of their stalks stick below this traced pencil line. Let the flowers and grasses at the ends of the row extend a little way beyond the lines you traced on the sides. When you put the mat over the picture it will cover the stem ends and the very ends of the row. It will look as though you had framed a small bit of flowery meadow.

There are so many different ways of designing flower pictures and so many different kinds of plants to use that you could make dozens of pictures and never make two that looked alike. You will also find that you can make pictures more and more easily as you practice doing it. Your designs will get better too, and soon you will be making pictures that are real works of art.

5
PROTECTING YOUR FLOWER PICTURES

Pressed, dried plants are very brittle, so if you want to keep your picture for any length of time you should protect it to keep the flowers from breaking or becoming dusty. The plants on herbarium sheets are protected by being kept in a folder or an album. Unlike most greeting cards, which have the picture on the outside, cards decorated with pressed flowers should be made so that a flap of the card folds over the picture. Pictures that are to hang on the wall or be used to decorate such things as place mats or boxes should be covered with a transparent material such as plastic or glass.

52

USING PLASTIC FILM

Covering your picture with a sheet of plastic film is one of the easiest ways to protect it. For this purpose you can use the kind of thin, flexible, transparent polyethylene film that is popular for wrapping food. Your mother probably has some that she will let you use, or you can buy a roll of it at the grocery store. These rolls are only twelve or eighteen inches wide, but that is wide enough to cover most pictures.

If you plan to cover your picture with this kind of film you should glue the plant material to cardboard that does not bend very easily. If the cardboard is thin the picture will warp when the film is pulled tightly over it. The cardboard should be at least two inches narrower than the plastic film. If you are using twelve-inch-wide plastic film you should make your picture no more than ten inches wide.

The picture should be completely dry before you cover it, since the plastic film will not let any moisture escape.

In addition to plastic film you will need a roll of sticky tape to fasten the edges of the film to the back of the cardboard. Cellophane tape or masking tape will serve this purpose.

Protecting Your Flower Pictures

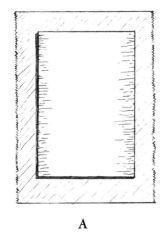

A

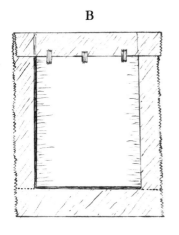

B

First tear or cut from the roll a piece of plastic film big enough to completely cover your picture and extend an extra inch or two beyond its edges. Lay the piece of film on a clean piece of newspaper or paper toweling. The film should be as flat and smooth as possible. Now lay the picture facedown in the center of the film (see illustration A).

Next prepare some short pieces of sticky tape. You will need at least three pieces of tape about one inch long for each side of your picture. Cut at least three pieces of tape this length. Stick one end of each piece of tape lightly to the bare edge of the table on which you are working. You will then be able to pull the tape off the table with one hand without letting go of the edge of the plastic film you will be holding in position with the other hand.

Now fold one of the free edges of the film around the edge of the cardboard. Hold this edge of film tightly and evenly against the entire edge of the cardboard and fasten it to the back of the picture with the pieces of sticky tape. If you stick down the middle of the edge of film first and then the two ends, it will be easier to fasten the film evenly. Stick two or three more pieces of tape along the edge of the film if you do not think three pieces are enough to hold it firmly (see illustration B).

Prepare three more pieces of tape to fasten the *opposite*

54

edge of film to the back of the picture. Pull gently on the middle of this edge as you fold it up so that the plastic will be stretched smoothly and tightly over the flower picture on the underside of the cardboard. Do not pull too hard, though, or you will bend the cardboard out of shape. Fasten the film to the back of the cardboard with tape, sticking down the middle first (see illustration C).

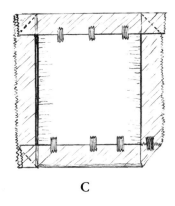

C

When these two opposite sides of the film are firmly fastened to the back of the picture, turn your picture over to see if the film is smooth. If it is too tight or not smooth, loosen the tape on one edge so you can adjust it. You may need fresh pieces of tape to fasten the edge down again.

When you are satisfied, put the picture facedown again and fasten the other two edges of the film. Finish one edge at a time. First fold in the corners as though you were wrapping a package. It will be easier to make neat corners if you stick down this triangular fold with a short piece of sticky tape you have prepared ahead of time. After the corners are turned in, fold the flap of film up over the edge of the cardboard and fasten it down with at least three pieces of tape. Fold over the last edge and fasten it in the same way (see illustration D).

D

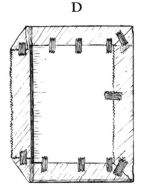

Check the front of the picture again and make any necessary adjustments. You should next seal the edges of

55

the plastic film to the back of the picture. Do this by covering them with long pieces of tape. It does not matter if the back of the picture looks a little messy, since it will not be seen. Sealing the edges of the film to the back of the picture will keep out dust and moisture. It will also hold the edges more firmly (see illustration E).

If you plan to hang your picture on the wall you will have to fasten a string across the back to make a hanger. Instructions for doing this are on page 69.

USING SEMIRIGID PLASTIC

Thin, flexible plastic film is strong enough to protect most flower pictures, but for some purposes you will need tougher material. You can buy clear semirigid polyethylene plastic that is very tough. It can be used to cover pictures that are going to be used as place mats, hot plates, or trays. The plastic will not be harmed even if you put on it a hot metal baking dish that has just come out of a 400-degree oven.

This kind of plastic is quite expensive and not always easy to find in stores. It is used instead of glass for covering such things as greenhouses, sun porches, and chickenhouse windows and can usually be bought in building-supply stores. Some hardware stores also have it for sale.

It usually comes in rolls that are three feet wide. You will have to buy a piece that is the whole width of the roll but you can have it cut to any length you want. This kind of plastic comes in various thicknesses. The kind that is five mills thick is thick enough for most purposes and is much less expensive than the ten-mills-thick variety.

You can fasten semirigid plastic over your picture in the same way described for covering a picture with flexible plastic film. But this stiffer plastic does not fold as easily, and it is sometimes difficult to make the corners neat and tight when you fold the edges over onto the back of the picture. It is better, therefore, to cut a sheet of semirigid plastic exactly the same size as the picture and seal the edges of the plastic and the picture together with strips of sticky tape.

You can seal the edges of your picture with masking tape or freezer tape. Freezer tape looks exactly like masking tape but is stronger and more waterproof. Another excellent product for sealing together the edges of pictures is a self-stick, plastic-coated cloth tape that comes in several different colors. It is very strong and completely waterproof.

All these tapes come in different widths. Use three-quarter-inch tape for sealing together the edges of small pictures. The wider one-and-a-half-inch tape looks better around the edges of large pictures.

You can use narrow widths of any of these tapes to seal the edges of very small narrow pictures (such as those you use to make bookmarks), or you can use strips of self-stick transparent plastic tape, which is only half an inch wide. This is a special transparent tape that is stronger than regular cellophane tape and does not get yellow and crack with age.

You can buy all these kinds of tape in rolls at most hardware stores and in some department stores, stationery stores, and supermarkets.

First cut the sheet of plastic exactly the same size as your picture. The easiest way of doing this is to lay the picture facedown on the plastic and trace around it. Regular lead pencil will not mark on smooth plastic, but you can use a dark-colored wax crayon, a felt pen or marker, or a china marking pencil that has a special sticky lead.

Cut the plastic with a sharp pair of scissors along the inside edge of the lines you have traced. You can clean off any marks left on the edge of the plastic with cleaning powder dampened with just a little water. Rinse the powder off thoroughly and dry the plastic before using it.

58

Protecting Your Flower Pictures

You should always make sure, before you fasten the plastic covering over your picture, that it has no dirt or finger marks on it. You will not be able to clean the inside surface of the plastic after it is fastened down.

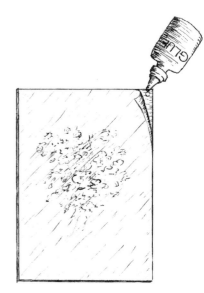

It will be easier to seal the edges of your picture if you fasten the sheet of plastic to it with a spot of glue in each corner before you put on the tape. Use the creamy kind of white glue that dries clear.

Place your picture faceup on a piece of newspaper and fit the plastic covering over it. Make sure the edges are even. Now raise the corners of the plastic one at a time, put a tiny dab of glue on each corner of the picture, and press the corner of the plastic sheet down on this spot of glue. Weight down the corners until the glue is dry. This will take about half an hour.

Sticking the strips of tape evenly around the edges of your picture is a rather tricky job. You should attach the tape to the plastic first and then fold it over onto the back. It is also best to finish sealing one edge before sticking tape onto another edge of the plastic.

Before you put a strip of tape along the edge of your picture you must mark this edge so that the tape will be even and in a straight line. Start by marking the top edge. Lay a ruler along the side of the picture so that its top

59

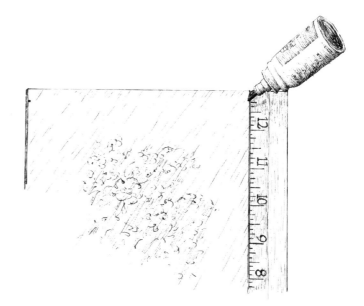

end is even with the top edge of the picture. Then with your crayon, felt pen, or china marking pencil make a tiny spot on the very margin of the plastic to indicate the right distance from the top edge. If you are using three-quarter-inch tape or half-inch tape, this mark will be a quarter of an inch from the top edge of the picture. Make the mark three quarters of an inch from the top edge of your picture if you are using tape that is one and a half inches wide.

Measure down from the top of your picture on the opposite side in the same way and mark it also. You should now have two tiny marks on the side edges of your picture that are exactly the same distance from the top edge.

The next step is to prepare a piece of tape to stick along the top edge. Peel a section of tape off the roll but do not cut it off yet. Hold the free end of the tape in one hand and the roll in the other hand and stretch the strip of tape in the air a few inches above the top edge of the picture. Pull more tape off the roll if you need it. The piece of tape should be two or three inches longer than the edge you want to stick it to. When you have peeled off a piece that is the right length, stick the free end of the tape to the bare edge of a tabletop and cut the strip off the roll. You will now have a strip the right length hanging from the edge of the table, ready to use.

Lay your picture faceup on a clean, hard, smooth surface such as a bare tabletop or kitchen counter. Take the hanging end of the strip of tape you have prepared in one hand and pull it up into the air so that the other end peels off the edge of the table. Take this second end in your other hand and hold the tape flat and tightly stretched between your two hands so it does not sag. Lower the strip, sticky-side-down, onto the top edge of the picture. Do this slowly and carefully so that you can place it exactly in the right position on the edge of the plastic. The bottom edge of the tape should just cover the two marks you made on the side edges of the plastic

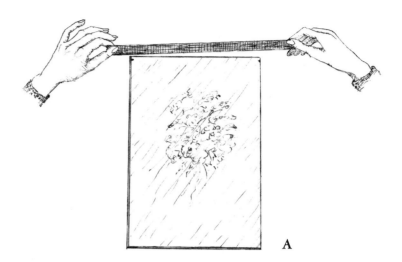

A

sheet. About half the width of the tape will be on the plastic, and half will be hanging over the edge of the picture. (See illustration A.)

You may find it easier to get the strip in position if you do not try to put both ends down on the marks at the same time. Lay one end of the strip in position on its mark before you lower the other end all the way down.

When the tape is correctly placed, press the two ends lightly to the tabletop on either side of the picture. Then run your fingers over the part of the tape that is on the plastic. This will stick it down smoothly and firmly. Try not to press down on the edge of the tape that is hanging over the edge of the picture onto the tabletop.

Now loosen one of the tape ends that are stuck to the table. Pull up on this end slowly. The strip of tape will

62

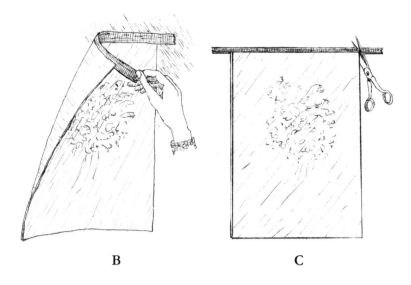

B

C

peel off the table but stay stuck along the upper edge of your picture. (See illustration B.)

Turn the picture facedown so that the free edge of the tape along the edge of the picture is sticky-side-up. Fold this sticky edge carefully over the edge of the picture and press it to the back. With a sharp pair of scissors trim off the two tabs of folded tape projecting from either side. (See illustration C.)

Next seal the bottom edge of your picture in the same manner. Then seal the two side edges. Mark each edge before putting on the tape and always stick the strip to the front of your picture first.

Instructions for making a hanger on the back of the picture are on page 69.

FRAMING YOUR PICTURE BEHIND GLASS

Pictures that you are planning to frame behind glass can be made on heavy white drawing paper or oak tag. It is wise to buy the kind of picture frame that comes with glass and a cardboard backing already fitted into the frame. You can usually buy small, simple frames of this kind for a dollar or two in department stores.

Always buy the frame before you make the picture to ensure that the picture will fit into the frame. Take the cardboard backing out of the frame and use it as a pattern to get your background paper the right size.

Some picture frames come with a mat between the glass and the cardboard backing. A mat is a piece of cardboard with its center cut out. It fits between the glass and the picture and makes an extra margin around the picture. A mat is not necessary but it makes most pictures look better when they are framed. It also keeps the glass from pressing tightly against the flowers if they are a little bumpy. White mats or mats of very soft colors look best around flower pictures.

If your frame comes with a mat you should take it out and trace the outline of the opening in the mat onto

64

your background paper. Lay the mat on the background paper so that the edges of the mat and the paper are exactly even. Trace very lightly around the edge of the opening with a pencil. This pencil outline will act as a guide for placing your design. When the picture is framed only plants glued inside the outline will show through the opening in the mat. You can erase the line after the picture is finished.

Be sure the glass is clean and dry on both sides before you put your picture into the frame. After this has been done you will not be able to wipe off any fingerprints or dust.

When you are sure the glass is clean, lay the picture frame, with the glass in it, upside down on the table. If there is a mat this should next be fitted against the glass. Then place the flower picture facedown on top of the

How a picture fits in a frame

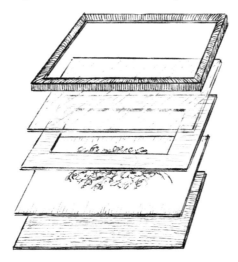

mat. If you do not use a mat, the picture goes facedown directly on top of the glass.

At this point it is a good idea to turn the frame over to see if everything has been correctly placed. Hold the picture and glass in position with one hand when you do this. After you have checked, you can slip the cardboard backing into the back of the frame.

Some picture frames are made so that the cardboard backing will slide up into a slot around the back edge of the frame. But in most frames the backing is held in place with little nails or triangular metal points. A small pair of pliers will help push the nails or points tightly into the inside edge of the frame. They should be pushed in very firmly and lie flat against the cardboard backing so that all the layers inside the frame are tightly held against each other. If you are using this kind of frame it is a good idea to cover the cracks between the frame and the backing with strips of masking tape. This will help hold the backing in place. It will also keep dust from coming through the cracks.

Pictures framed behind glass are usually hung from a piece of wire stretched across the back between two little screw eyes. If your frame does not come equipped with wire and screw eyes you can get them at the hardware store.

Back of framed picture

66

Measure down about two inches from the top of the back of the frame, and make marks on the back edges on both sides. These marks should be the same distance from the top edge. Screw the screw eyes into the frame where the marks are.

Cut some picture wire about three inches longer than the width of the frame and put the ends through the two screw eyes. Bend these ends back toward the middle of the picture and twist them tightly several times around the wire that is extended between the two screw eyes. The wire need not be stretched tightly across the back of the picture, but it should not be so loose that the center will pull up above the top edge of the frame. Be sure the wire is firmly twisted so it will not pull out of the screw eyes.

SPRAYING YOUR PICTURE WITH LIQUID PLASTIC

If you do not cover your picture with glass or a sheet of plastic, you can spray it with transparent liquid plastic to protect the dried flowers from dust. This coating will also keep the flowers from being rubbed off the background to which they are glued, and it will help to keep the colors from fading. Flower pictures that are going to be sprayed should be made on fairly stiff cardboard.

You can buy spray cans of transparent liquid plastic in most art-supply stores and in some stationery and hardware stores. Be sure to follow the directions on the can.

It is best to use spray outdoors or in a room with a partly open window. If you do your spraying indoors, you should put several large sheets of newspaper behind the picture. This will prevent any plastic that sprays beyond the edges of the picture from getting on the furniture, rug, or floor.

Hold the spray can about one foot or a little farther away from the picture. Move the can up and down and back and forth as you spray so that the whole picture will be coated evenly. Do not use too much spray at one time or in one place, because this will make the spray pool and run and make spots on the picture. Several light coats are better than one heavy coat. Let each coat dry for a few minutes before spraying on another.

Never point the spray can toward your own face or at anyone else. Always be sure that the spray hole is pointing away from you before you press down on the button.

It is a good idea to tie a large handkerchief over your nose and mouth so that you do not breathe in the spray.

68

A HANGER FOR YOUR PICTURE

If you want to hang an unframed picture on the wall you will have to fasten a string across the back. You can do this with short pieces of strong sticky tape. The string should be a little longer than the width of the picture.

Measure down about two inches from the top of the picture on either side and make marks on the back. These marks should be the same distance from the top edge and about an inch in from the side edges. They will show where the two ends of the string should be fastened.

Tie a big knot in each end of the string. Then lay the string loosely across the back of the picture with these knots on the marks you made. The string between the knots should loop up toward, but should not come above, the top edge of the picture. If there is too much string, cut a little off one end and tie another knot at this end. Test it until you have it the right length.

Cut off two short pieces of sticky tape and place them across the string *above* the knots. Press the tape down firmly. The knots below the strips of tape will prevent the string from coming loose when the weight of the picture is on it.

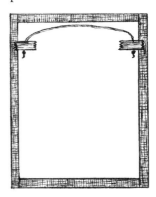

Back of plastic-covered picture

69

6
THINGS TO MAKE
AND DECORATE WITH
PRESSED FLOWERS

You can do other things with pressed plants besides using them in herbariums or making them into pictures to hang on the wall. Articles decorated with pressed flowers are pretty, fun to make, and wonderful gifts.

GREETING CARDS

A greeting card that you have made and decorated yourself with a flower picture is an excellent birthday card for your mother, grandparents, or aunts. Greeting cards are also good presents to give on Valentine's Day, Mother's Day, Christmas, and Easter.

The picture on a greeting card can be a simple spray or bouquet of dainty flowers and grasses, or you can make your design more original. A wreath shaped like a heart would be suitable for Valentine's Day. A Christmas tree made from the tip of a fern frond decorated with tiny flowers and single petals would be attractive on a Christmas card.

Suggestions for designs and the methods of making pictures are given in the chapter called "Pressed Flower Pictures." You should not use more than three layers of plants on a greeting card. These plants should be pressed very flat so that the design will not be too bumpy. Egg-white glue is best for fastening down the small bits of plant material that are suitable for greeting cards. Hold the little pieces of plant with tweezers and coat the backs thoroughly with egg-white glue before laying them in position.

Heavy white drawing paper, heavy letter paper, or oak tag are all suitable for making greeting cards. You should make a folded card with the flower picture on one of the inside pages. The other half of the card will fold over the picture to protect it so that you do not need to spray it with liquid plastic or cover it with plastic film. You can write on the outside of the folded card and also on the page opposite the picture.

Before you start designing your picture, cut the paper the size and shape you want your finished card to be.

71

If you are not going to mail the card, you do not have to worry about having an envelope into which it will fit. You can then make the card any size or shape you want. If you plan to mail your card, you will have to make one that fits into a ready-made envelope unless you also want to make an envelope of the right size.

If you decide on a ready-made envelope use it as a pattern to get the card the right size. First fold the paper you are planning to use for your card in half. Then lay the envelope on the paper so that one edge of the envelope is even with the fold. Trace lightly around the other three sides of the envelope. Then cut through both layers of the folded paper a little way inside this outline. Test the folded card to make sure it slips easily into the envelope. Trim off the edges a little if necessary.

If you plan to make your own envelope, first cut your card to the desired shape and size so you can use it as a pattern for the envelope. The piece of paper you will

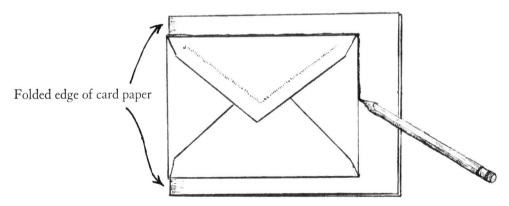

Folded edge of card paper

Trace around envelope to
draw outline of card

need for the envelope should be at least two inches wider and two inches longer than the open card. Letter paper or typewriter paper makes good envelopes.

Fold your envelope paper in half. Then lay the folded card on top of it so that one edge of the card is even with the fold in the envelope paper. There should be one to two inches of the folded envelope paper projecting beyond the other edges of the card (see diagram A, page 74).

Trace lightly around these three edges of the card. Then, if necessary, trim off enough of the edges of the folded envelope paper so that the margins outside the traced outline are between one and two inches wide. Be sure they are at least one inch wide.

Now open up the envelope paper and draw pencil lines a quarter of an inch outside of and parallel to the outline of the card. Use a ruler to measure and draw these lines. Next snip in along the crease to the ends of this outside set of lines and cut off the margin surrounding the outer lines. You should only trim the margins off half the unfolded envelope paper (see diagram B, page 74).

Now fold the trimmed part back onto the untrimmed half of the envelope paper. With a pencil and ruler make a diagonal line across each corner of the untrimmed half of the folded paper (see diagram C). Snip these triangular

73

Things to Make with Pressed Flowers

A

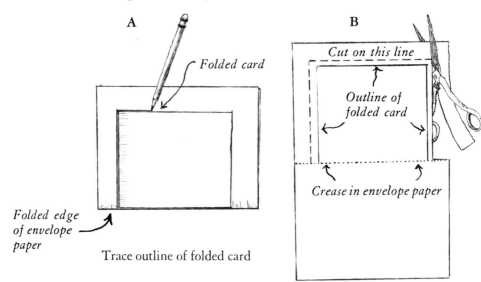

Folded card

Folded edge
of envelope
paper

Trace outline of folded card

B

Cut on this line

Outline of
folded card

Crease in envelope paper

Cut off part of margin
outside outline of card

C

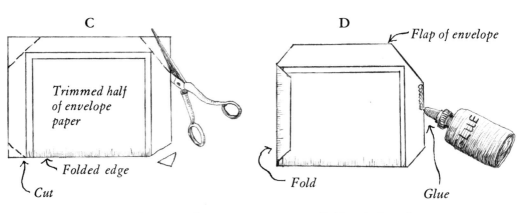

Trimmed half
of envelope
paper

Folded edge

Cut

Mark and cut off corners of
untrimmed half of envelope
paper

D

Flap of envelope

Fold

GLUE

Glue

Fold and glue tabs to
finish envelope

pieces off the corners. Be careful not to cut into the corners of the other, trimmed half. You will now have a piece of folded paper a little bigger than your folded card, with tabs of paper sticking out on three sides. Fold these tabs over the edges of the trimmed half of the paper. Put a little glue on the two tabs that are on opposite sides of the envelope and fasten them down (see diagram D). The third tab is the flap of the envelope. Do not put glue on it until you have put the finished card inside.

When the glue on the two tabs is dry, slip your card into the envelope to see if it fits. Trim off the edges of the card if it does not slide in easily.

BOOKMARKS

Flower pictures that are going to be used as bookmarks should be glued onto heavy drawing paper or oak tag. Cut a strip of paper an inch and three quarters wide and six to seven inches long. Draw an outline before you cut this strip. Use a ruler to measure the width and length and get the lines straight. The corner of a book, pad, or magazine will help you to get the corners square.

Because a bookmark is so narrow, the most suitable design is a garland. You can use any number of different

Bookmark

small flowers, leaves, grasses, and single flower petals to make your garlands so each bookmark can be different. Use egg-white glue to fasten them down, and coat their backs thoroughly before laying them in position. A pair of tweezers will make it easier for you to hold the little pieces of plant while you apply the glue. Two or three layers of plants are enough.

It is best to cover a bookmark picture with a strip of semirigid plastic. Seal the edges together with transparent plastic sticky tape. If you cannot get any semirigid plastic you can cover the picture by folding thin plastic film over it, but this will not be as strong.

No matter what kind of plastic you use to cover your bookmark picture, you should cover the back of the bookmark with a strip of freezer tape or self-stick, plastic-coated cloth tape an inch and a half wide. The directions for covering pictures with semirigid plastic or plastic film have been given in the previous chapter.

PLACE MATS AND COASTERS

Place mats and coasters are made much the same way as bookmarks except that coasters are usually about three or four inches square and place mats are much bigger.

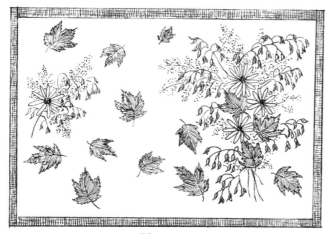
Place mat

They are usually about eighteen inches long and twelve inches wide.

You can use heavy drawing paper or oak tag as the background for a flower picture that is going to be used as a coaster or place mat. Or you may use heavier cardboard.

Coasters and place mats should be sealed behind pieces of semirigid plastic. Seal the edges of place mats together with one-and-a-half-inch-wide freezer tape or self-stick, plastic-coated cloth tape. Use three-quarter-inch tape for sealing the edges of coasters.

In addition to protecting the tops of the pictures you make for coasters and place mats, you should protect the undersides. Coasters and place mats get things spilled on them and have to be cleaned off with a damp cloth. For

77

Coasters

this reason you should cover the underside of your background paper or cardboard with waterproof plastic. Since this need not be transparent, you can use the kind of self-adhesive vinyl plastic that is used to cover shelves and kitchen tables.

This kind of vinyl comes in rolls and is usually about eighteen inches wide. It comes in a variety of colors and can be bought in most hardware and department stores and supermarkets. The sticky side of the vinyl is covered with a protective paper backing that must be peeled off. The paper backing is marked out in one-inch squares, which makes it easy to measure and cut in a straight line.

Cover the back of your background paper or cardboard with vinyl before you glue plants to the front. First cut the paper the size you want it. You should make coasters and place mats either square or rectangular so the edges can be easily sealed with tape. Cut a piece of the vinyl about one inch longer and one inch wider than your picture.

Lay the vinyl paper-side-up on a bare table. It will curl a little but do not let this worry you. You are now ready to peel off the paper backing so that the sticky side is exposed. The paper backing on most kinds of self-adhesive plastic is split down the middle, which makes it easier

78

to peel off. Hold the upper edge of the sheet with one hand on each side of the split-line and bend the vinyl back from this line. This will loosen the edges of the split so you can grasp the corners of the backing paper and peel it off the plastic.

If the piece of vinyl you are using does not have a split-line across the paper backing, you can loosen the edge by holding the edge near one corner between the fingers of both hands. Twist the edge as though you were planning to tear it. The vinyl will not tear but the paper backing will tear a little and one corner of the torn edge will come unstuck. Twist the edge gently the other way to loosen the other corner of the tear. Peel back the edge of the paper backing until you have loosened it from the corner of the vinyl underneath. Then, starting at this corner, peel off all the backing so that the sticky side of the vinyl is completely exposed.

The vinyl should lie absolutely flat and smooth, sticky-side-up, on the table before you place your cardboard or paper on it. Hold the background paper right-side-up by the middle of two opposite edges and lower it carefully onto the sticky vinyl. You should have a narrow rim of vinyl projecting all around the edges of the background paper. Do not press down on any part of the background paper until it is lying flat and in the correct position on the vinyl. As long as you have not yet pressed it down you can usually pick up the paper from the vinyl again if you have to adjust its position.

When your background paper is in the correct position on the vinyl, press it down. Start pressing in the center and work toward the edges, rubbing gently with your fingers. Be sure your hands are clean and dry so that you do not make marks on the surface of the background paper. When the vinyl and background paper are stuck together everywhere, trim off the extra edges of vinyl with a pair of scissors.

Now turn the background paper over onto a clean piece of paper so that it is plastic-side-up, and rub it very firmly, starting in the center. If there are any bubbles of air under the vinyl, prick them with a pin to make a tiny hole. You can then force the air out from under the plastic by rubbing in from the edges of the bubble toward the pinprick. The point of the pin may go through the sheet of background paper, but do not let this bother you; the tiny pinhole will not show on the front side of your picture. If there are wrinkles in the plastic, rub them firmly so that the vinyl on each side of the wrinkle is tightly stuck down. Once the vinyl has been firmly fastened all over the bottom of the background paper, you are ready to design your flower picture on the front and glue it down.

Any small picture is suitable on a coaster. You must remember, however, that the plant material you use should lie very flat on the background. If you make your picture too thick and bumpy a glass that is put on the coaster will not sit firmly. For this reason you should only use material that is pressed really flat, and there should be no more than three layers of plants.

You can cover the whole area of a place mat with one big picture. Or, if you prefer, you can glue small groups of plants in the corners. You can also make a wreath around the edge. Remember that since the center of the mat will be covered by a plate, the design in that area will be hidden from view most of the time. You should also remember that the area about three quarters of an inch around the edge of the place mat or coaster will be

Place mat with decorated corners

Place mat decorated with wreath

covered by tape. Leave a margin at least an inch wide around the edge of your design.

When the picture on your place mat or coaster is complete and thoroughly dry, seal it behind a piece of semirigid plastic as explained on pages 56–63.

HOT PLATES

Hot plates should be covered with semirigid plastic that will withstand heat. Transparent semirigid polyethylene plastic, either five or ten mills thick, is suitable for this purpose. You will also need self-stick, plastic-coated cloth tape, an inch and a half wide, to seal the edges.

The back of the hot plate should be covered with flannel, felt, or a piece of thin, heatproof plastic foam. It is usually possible to get any of these materials with self-sticking adhesive on the back. The sticky side is covered with a kind of waxy paper that peels off to expose the adhesive.

These materials are usually available in most department and hardware stores and in some supermarkets, but only in rather narrow pieces, about six inches wide and eighteen inches long. They are large enough to cover the backs of most hot plates, which are usually six to seven inches square. If you wish, you can buy a piece of felt at an ordinary yard-goods store, cut it to the right size, and fasten it to the back of the hot plate with the kind of all-purpose glue that can be used to stick things to plastic.

A hot plate should be made of several layers of cardboard because it must be thick enough to protect the table-top from the heat of the hot dishes placed on it. Three cardboards, each one about as thick as the lid of a strong gift box, are usually enough. This will make your hot plate about a quarter of an inch thick by the time you have covered it with semirigid plastic and put felt, flannel, or plastic foam on the back.

Cut three pieces of cardboard the size you want your hot plate to be. They should all be exactly the same size. Use the first piece you cut as a pattern and trace around it to make the other two. If your cardboard is not white, you should also cut to size a piece of white drawing paper. You can then glue this paper to the top of your layers of cardboard as a background for your picture.

Glue the pieces of cardboard together first. Lay the bottom piece on a sheet of newspaper and smear one side of it with all-purpose glue or paste. Be sure the corners and edges are gluey. Fit the second piece of cardboard over this gluey side so the edges are exactly together. Put one

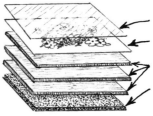

A hot plate is made of several layers

Semirigid plastic

Picture

Cardboard

Felt, flannel, or heatproof plastic foam

or two heavy books on top, and let the glue dry for about ten minutes. Smear more glue on one side of the third piece of cardboard and fit it on top of the pile. Weight it down and let it dry. If you need to glue a piece of white paper on top of your layers of cardboard, put this on next.

You should keep your sandwich of cardboard pressed under a weight to dry for at least two hours before mounting your plant material.

When you have designed and glued down your picture, and it is completely and thoroughly dry, seal a piece of semirigid transparent plastic over it with plastic-coated cloth tape an inch and a half wide. Follow the directions for doing this on pages 56–63.

After you have sealed the plastic over your picture, you should stick a piece of felt, flannel, or heatproof plastic foam to the underside of the hot plate. Cut the piece of material a little larger than the hot plate. You can trim off the extra edges after the material has been fastened on.

In addition to the articles already mentioned you can decorate other objects with pressed plants. A sturdy box with a flower picture on the lid can be used to hold jewelry or other precious things. Or you can glue a flower picture

Finished hot plate

84

Heavenly bamboo

(*Nandina domestica*). These should be cut when the
berries are red. The berries of privet (*Ligustrum*) will stay
either green or dark blue depending on the color of the
fruit when the branches are cut. Fire thorn (*Pyracantha
coccinea*) has orange, scarlet, yellow, or sometimes pink

Common privet

Fire thorn

Beauty-berry

Bayberry

fruit. Beauty-berry (*Callicarpa purpurea*) has berries of a beautiful bright violet. Be sure to wear leather gloves while handling the prickly branches of fire thorn or barberry.

The waxy gray-green berries of bayberry (*Myrica pensylvanica*) are lovely in winter bouquets. They grow in thick clusters a little way down from the tips of the branches, so snip off the part above the berries before you dry them. Bayberries are most plentiful along the seashore, and early settlers discovered that they could make candle wax out of the fruits.

Black alder, which is really a holly (*Ilex verticillata*) that loses its leaves, has bright red berries. The true alders (*Alnus*) have seed capsules that look rather like miniature pine cones scattered in groups along their branches. These seed capsules can be picked and dried when they are green or brown as long as they are firm.

The seed capsules and seed heads of many plants other than shrubs can be dried for winter flower arrangements. The feathery seed heads of clematis are beautiful when dried. They should be picked before they become really fluffy. Clematis is both the botanical name and the common name for a group of plants. Some of the other common names for the pretty vines in this genus are traveler's joy, love vine, and virgin's bower.

90

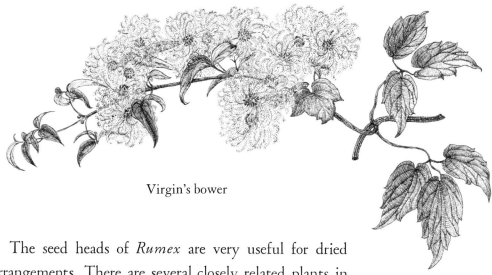

Virgin's bower

The seed heads of *Rumex* are very useful for dried arrangements. There are several closely related plants in this group of common weeds, all of which are usually called dock or sorrel. They carry showy seed heads on the top of stout stalks. These can be gathered when they are still green or after they have started to turn color. They will stay green, rosy red, or mahogany brown, depending on the color they were when you dried them.

True alder

Black alder

Common milkweed pods

Preserving Plants for Arrangements

The pods of all the milkweeds (*Asclepias*) are very handsome when they are dried. Pick these in late fall when they are plump but before they open. You can usually judge the right time to cut a milkweed by pressing gently on the edges of the crease that runs the length of the pod. If these edges can be pulled apart with gentle pressure, the pods are ready to pick. The seed pods and seed capsules of poppies, peonies, yucca such as Adam's needle, irises, and lilies are also useful for winter bouquets.

The fruiting capsules of the sensitive fern (*Onoclea sensibilis*) look like a double row of beads at the tip of the stalk. For this reason this fern is sometimes called the bead fern. The fruiting fronds of ostrich fern (*Matteuccia struthiopteris*), which resemble short, curly feathers, give this fern its common name. Both these plants will last for years in dried arrangements.

Swamps and marshes are full of sedges, cattails, and rushes that have wonderfully decorative seed heads. Most grain plants—such as wheat, rye, millet, oats, and barley —also have beautiful seed heads, as do many of the wild grasses. These are all best picked just as the seed heads start to turn color.

The cobs of most varieties of corn are too large to be useful in winter bouquets, though the tassels can be cut

Fertile frond of sensitive
fern

and dried. But the small, round heads of shiny yellow or deep red grains of popcorn are excellent in arrangements. Corn tassels should be cut just as they start to turn golden. The grains of popcorn should be fully ripened and hard before the cobs are cut. Okra pods and the seed heads of onion and garlic can also be gathered and dried when they turn color. The soft orange-red lanterns of the Chinese lantern plant (*Physalis franchetii*), also called ground cherry, are colorful accents in dried bouquets.

These are just a few of the plants that have decorative fruits suitable for drying. You will undoubtedly be able to find many others in the garden and in the wild that you can dry and use as decoration. It is best to cut most seed heads just as they are beginning to ripen, but before they open and spill their seeds. This is usually when they start turning brown or yellow.

When you get your stalks home, strip off all the leaves. These will just shrivel up anyway. It is a good idea to peel back the husk that encloses a cob of popcorn immediately, while it is pliable. Peel each leafy section down carefully, but leave it attached to the base of the cob. Trim off the ragged tips with a pair of scissors. When the sections of husk are dry they will stand out around the cob like pale yellow petals.

93

Fertile frond of ostrich fern

Marsh rushes, sedges, and grasses

Popcorn cob

Yucca seed pod

Yucca

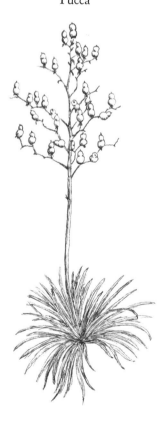

Branches and stiff, thick stems can be dried by standing them upright in an empty jar or pail. Most grasses,
grains, and rushes can also be dried in an upright position.
Plants that have thin, weak stalks are best dried by laying
them flat on sheets of newspaper in a warm, airy place.
Do not pile them on top of each other.

If you do not have enough room to spread out such
plants, you can hang them up to dry. Gather them into
bunches and wrap a strong elastic band around their stems
a few inches from the bottom. Be sure the elastic band is
tightly wound around the stems because they will shrink
as they dry. Fasten a loop of string to the elastic band
and hang the bunch upside down from a nail, hook, or
coat hanger in a warm, dry place such as an attic or closet.

Milkweed pods are best dried by placing the stalks
head down in a large paper bag with the stems sticking
out at the top. Crush the top of the bag around the stalks
and tie it tightly together with a long string. Tie the loose
ends of the string together to make a loop and hang the
bag up for three or four weeks.

94

Preserving Plants for Arrangements

You will want to check the condition of the pods once in a while. One day you will see that they are beginning to split open and that the white silk is puffing out. Take the bag outdoors before you unwrap the pods because the silk is so light it will blow all over. Clean the silk and the seeds out of the pods with your fingers. Be careful not to tear the pods. When the pods are empty, stand the stalks upright in an empty jar until they become stiff and dry.

Sumac and bayberry often have small insects hidden among the fruit. You should get rid of these insects or they will ruin the berries. A good way to do this is to put about a third of a cupful of strong moth flakes in the bottom of a large paper bag. Cover the flakes loosely with a paper towel. Put the branches into the bag upside down. Tie the bag tightly closed and hang it up in the same way suggested for milkweed pods. Do not open it for three or four weeks. By then the gas from the moth flakes will have killed the insects.

The flowers as well as the fruits of many plants can be dried for arrangements either by laying the stalks on newspaper to dry or by hanging them upside down in bunches in a warm, dry place.

Pussy willows dry beautifully if you cut the branches and stand them in an empty vase. These should be cut

Early goldenrod

when the pussies have crept out from under the brown bud scale and grown fat but while they are still soft with gray fur.

The blossoming heads of silverrods and goldenrods are easily dried. Pearly everlasting (*Anaphalis margaritacea*) is also excellent for winter bouquets. This native plant grows mostly in poor, sandy soil. The stems and leaves are matted with cottony white hairs and the blossoms are puffs of fluffy silver-white. All these should be picked just as the buds begin to open.

Large thistles (*Cirsium*) may also be dried if they are picked when the points of purple hair are just beginning to push through the tops of the green buds. Globe thistles (*Echinops*) should be gathered as the steel blue flowers first open. Teasel (*Dipsacus*) should be picked after the rows of tiny flowers on the prickly heads have finished blooming.

Be sure to wear heavy leather gloves to protect your hands when you handle teasel, thistles, or globe thistles. The spines on the stems and leaves hurt dreadfully when they stick your fingers. Take off the leaves and prickles while they are still green by pulling the stalks through a wad of cloth.

There are several kinds of *Eupatorium* called joe-pye

Pussy willow

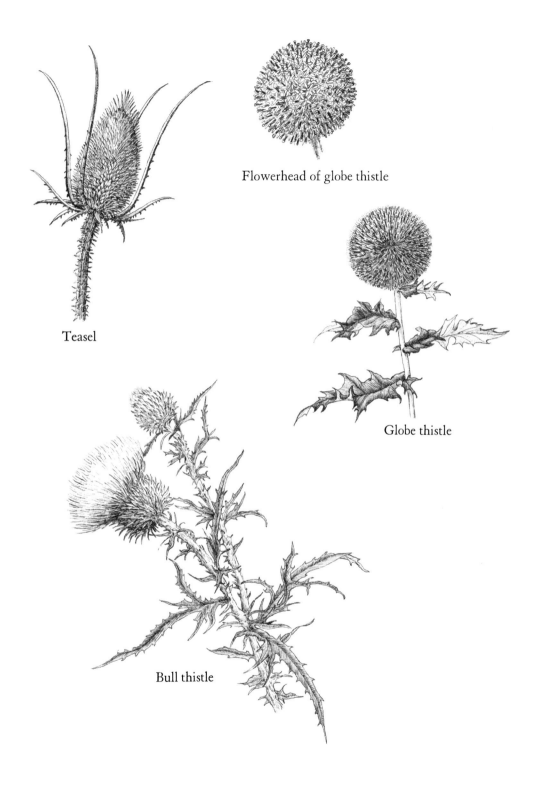

Flowerhead of globe thistle

Teasel

Globe thistle

Bull thistle

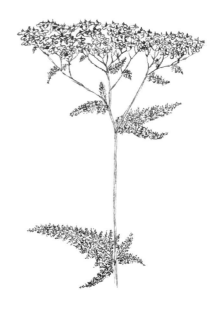

Spotted joe-pye weed   Common yarrow

weed. Their rather flat heads of rose-pink flowers can be
dried if they are picked when the buds are pink but before
they open. The yarrows (*Achillea*) also have excellent
flowers for drying. The common wild yarrow usually has
flat heads of rather dingy white flowers, but many of the
yarrows that are grown in gardens are much more decorative. Some of these have glistening white flowers; others
are rosy pink or a lovely soft golden yellow. It is best to
pick both the wild yarrow and the garden yarrows just
as the buds in the flower head start to open.

98

 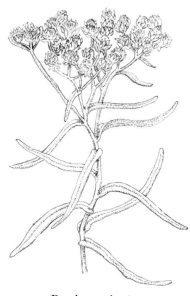

Tansy   Pearly everlasting

Tansy (*Tanacetum vulgare*) is not really a native wild
flower, though it often grows wild in fields and along
roadsides in New England. Tansy was originally brought
to this country by the early pioneers as a useful herb, and
it escaped from their gardens. Before the days of refrigera-
tion stalks of tansy were put in the closet where meat was
stored, to keep it from spoiling. It was also used, and still
can be used, to repel insects, which do not like its bitter,
spicy smell. The dried blooms can be put in cheesecloth
bags and put in a drawer with woolens to keep out moths.
Flies and ants will not crawl over food that is surrounded
with a wreath of tansy. However, you should not eat the
wreath!

99

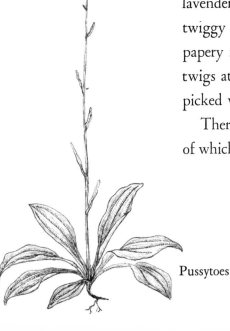

Rabbit-foot clover

Pussytoes

Preserving Plants for Arrangements

The flowers of tansy are flat-topped clusters of bright yellow buttons. They should be gathered for drying as soon as they are yellow, since they become brownish very quickly if they are allowed to mature on the plant.

In addition to these taller weeds you can pick smaller wild flowers, which can be dried for little bouquets. Pussytoes (*Antennaria*) has pinky white tassels that grow in small clusters on the tips of rather woolly stems. These may grow a foot tall but are usually shorter. Some plants have almost pure white flowers; others have rosy pink "toes." Pick them just as the buds begin to open.

Rabbit-foot clover (*Trifolium arvense*) is another little plant that grows in poor, gravelly soil. It is a true clover and has small three-parted leaves. The blossoms look rather like grayish pink pussy willows. They should be picked as soon as they are furry.

If you live near the seacoast you can probably find sea lavender (*Limonium*) in the salt marshes. This is a twiggy little plant about twelve inches tall with small papery rosy purple flowers set in rows on the spreading twigs at the tip of the main stem. This plant should be picked when the flowers are fully open.

There are many different kinds of sea lavender, many of which are grown as garden plants. These are frequently

listed in seed catalogs as statice, and they are all wonderful for dried bouquets. Their loose heads of papery flowers are showier than those of the wild sea lavender and come in many different colors: yellow, lavender, lavender-blue, rosy reds, apricot pink, and white.

If you have a sunny corner where you can plant flowers you might like to grow some of these sea lavenders and also some of the other flowers that are especially good for making dried bouquets.

These are all annual flowers. Annuals are plants that live only one year but grow quickly from seeds planted in the spring so they will flower that same summer. Most annuals bloom all summer.

Most annuals are easy to grow in any ordinary garden soil. Follow the directions on the seed package and keep them watered and weeded. You can usually find the majority of these listed and illustrated in the catalogs of most seed companies. Some of these companies, to whom

Wild sea lavender

Statice

Immortelle

Globe amaranth

you can send for catalogs, are listed with their addresses in the back of this book.

Strawflowers (*Helichrysum*) and immortelles (*Xeranthemum*) both have large, papery, many-petaled flowers that look the same when they are dry as they do when they are fresh. They come in just about every color of the rainbow. Acroclinium (*Helipterum roseum*), sometimes called sunrays, also has papery flowers. These come in all shades of red and pink and in creamy white. Golden ageratum—which has fluffy heads of small, rich yellow flowers—is not really an ageratum at all. Its botanical name is *Lonas inodora*. All four of these flowers should be picked for drying just as the buds are beginning to open. The petals will keep unfurling as they dry.

Globe amaranth (*Gomphrena globosa*) is another colorful flower that dries well. It has clusters of small flowers in rather cloverlike heads. Most globe amaranths have white, reddish purple, pink, rose, or lavender flowers, but a few varieties are orange or creamy yellow. These should be grown in full sun and picked when the blossoms are fully open.

Your more colorful dried flowers can be mixed with the fascinating bells of Ireland or shellflowers, whose botanical name is *Moluccella laevis*. The petals of the flowers

are really tiny and white, but each blossom is surrounded by a soft, green, leafy bell that looks as if it were penciled with white lines. Bells of Ireland grow in long sprays that are beautiful in arrangements of either dried or fresh flowers. Wait until the bells are fully open before you pick them.

Bells of Ireland

Celosia is another annual that is easy to grow and dry. Many people think *Celosia* flowers are too big and gaudy for indoor arrangements and do not like them even in the garden. But they can be very handsome in a large jug in a simply decorated room with plain walls. Their colors are so brilliant, however, that they do not fit in well with every decorating scheme. A few *Celosia* flowers are white, but the blossoms are most often fire-engine red, brilliant orange, or deep yellow.

There are two main types of *Celosia*. One type is often called pampas plume. It has flowers that resemble bunches of soft feathers. The other type, called cockscomb, is as brilliantly colored as the first but quite different in shape and texture. The flowers are plushy and look a little like cauliflowers that have fallen into a pot of dye. There are a few dwarf forms of *Celosia*, but most of them grow three feet tall with plumes a foot long or with cockscombs the size of a small football.

Celosia, dwarf plume type

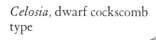

Celosia, dwarf cockscomb type

Hydrangea

Preserving Plants for Arrangements

In addition to these easily grown annuals several other garden plants have flowers that dry well for winter bouquets. Your mother may grow some of these in her garden. Hydrangea flowers, baby's breath (*Gypsophila paniculata*), sea thrift (*Armeria*), lavender, and astilbe and the heathers are garden plants, at least in this country. They can all be air-dried quite easily.

Experiment with plants that have heads or spikes of very tiny flowers. Brightly colored flowers usually keep their colors better than pale flowers. Most white blossoms tend to turn cream-colored as they dry.

All the flowers mentioned can be dried by hanging them upside down in bunches in a warm, dry place, just as you hang up seed heads. Unless the leaves are very small it is best to take them off the stems before drying them.

Sea thrift

Baby's breath with close-ups of clusters of single and double flowers

DRYING PLANTS IN DESICCANTS

Flowers with large, soft petals should not be air-dried because they lose their shapes as the petals shrivel up. Most leaves also curl and shrivel as they dry.

Flowers and leaves of this kind are best dried by burying them in a special mixture that quickly absorbs their moisture and at the same time supports them so they cannot change shape. Such mixtures are called desiccants.

You can dry many different kinds of flowers and leaves by burying them in desiccants, but some are more easily dried than others. Branches with small leaves dry better than those with larger leaves. Large, dry leaves are likely to break off the twigs when you arrange them. Green leaves will stay green after they are dried in desiccants as long as they are kept out of strong sunlight, but they are seldom as bright as they were when fresh. Dried fall foliage retains its brilliant color.

The easiest kinds of flowers to dry in desiccants are those with many layers of firm petals, such as roses, marigolds, zinnias, and chrysanthemums. Flowers with a single circle of petals, such as daisies, hollyhocks, and single dahlias, are also easy to dry by this method. Heads of blossoms made up of many small flowers, such as gerani-

Astilibe

Lavender

105

Heather

ums, butterfly weed, candytuft, and Queen Anne's lace, are not as easy to dry without mashing them out of shape. Neither are the flowering spikes of such plants as lilac, delphinium, salvia, and snapdragons. It is very difficult to dry tube-shaped or trumpet-shaped flowers, such as single petunias, morning glories, and trumpet daffodils.

Before you pick any plant material to be dried in desiccants, you should prepare the drying mixture. Flowers and leaves must be very fresh at the time they are buried.

There are several different mixtures that can be used for drying plants. One of the easiest to use is a combination of white cornmeal and powdered borax. You can buy both these ingredients in a grocery store. Powdered borax is used for cleaning. White cornmeal is used for baking and as a cooked cereal.

You will need a large bowl, pot, or pail in which to mix the borax and cornmeal. Five cups of white cornmeal thoroughly mixed with one cup of powdered borax will make enough desiccant to dry a few medium-sized flowers. If you plan to dry more than two or three blossoms at a time, you would be wise to mix up twice as much drying powder so that you will have enough to completely bury all your blossoms.

You can use this drying mixture over and over again

if you keep it in a tightly covered box in which it will stay dry. Be sure to label this container very clearly so your mother will not use it for cooking by mistake.

You can also dry flowers by burying them in perlite. This comes in large bags and is not expensive. You can usually buy perlite at hardware stores, garden centers, and stores that sell building supplies. Perlite is white and very light. The size of the grains is usually marked on the outside of the bag. Get fine- or medium-grained perlite for burying plants.

Use any fairly strong box *without* a cover to hold your plants when you bury them in either the cornmeal-borax mixture or in perlite.

You can also use a desiccant called silica gel for drying plants. It is not as dusty as the other two desiccants mentioned but it is much more expensive and not as easy to get. Some garden centers and hardware stores sell silica gel.

If you bury plants in silica gel you *must* seal them in a completely airtight box of tin or plastic with a tight-fitting lid. You will also have to dry out the silica gel after you have used it a few times. Always keep silica gel in a sealed airtight container when you are not using it or it will absorb moisture out of the air. Silica gel looks and

Grasses, oats, and wheat

Corn tassel

feels quite dry even when it is full of moisture. For this reason always buy the kind especially mixed for drying flowers. This kind has little blue specks mixed with the white grains. These specks stay blue as long as the silica gel is dry enough to use. When they disappear, dry the silica gel by putting it in an open pan in a 250-degree oven. Cans of silica gel used for drying flowers usually have directions for use printed on a slip of paper inside the can. Follow these directions exactly.

No matter what kind of desiccant you plan to use, have a suitable container ready for drying your plants before you pick them. You will not need a very big box for drying most flowers. You will cut off most of the stem and only bury the flower itself. This saves space and desiccant.

If you are going to use silica gel find a tin or plastic container with a tight-fitting lid. The tin should be at least six inches deep. If you are going to use perlite or a mixture of borax and cornmeal you should use an uncovered cardboard box. Choose a firmly made box of fairly stiff cardboard, or of corrugated cardboard if you wish. The box should be about four inches deep and big enough around to hold your plant without crushing it. A shoe box is big enough to hold most medium-sized flowers.

Preserving Plants for Arrangements

For your first experiment in drying flowers in a desiccant choose a blossom that is easy to dry and not too big. A type of flower with several layers of rather firm petals, such as a rose, zinnia, or marigold, is good to start with. Such flowers should be dried faceup in the box.

Cut off most of the stem, leaving only about three inches on the flower. If you are using silica gel you will probably have to cut off even more stem in order to fit the flower head and its stem in a closed box.

If you are using perlite or the borax-cornmeal mixture, the stem can stick out of the box. When you dry flower heads faceup in these mixtures you can make a hole in the bottom of the box just big enough for the three-inch-long stem to fit down through it. A big nail or turkey skewer is a good instrument for punching this hole. This means your box does not have to be very deep, and you will not have to use so much desiccant.

You will have to set up your box on blocks or books so that the bottom is about four inches above the surface on which it will be placed. Put the blocks under the ends of the box, leaving a space under the hole in the middle so that the stem can hang down through the hole. While you are covering the flower with desiccant you can prop up your box on any convenient table. While the flower

is drying you will probably want to keep the box in an out-of-the-way corner, since it should not be disturbed for a week or two. Be sure the box is always placed firmly on its props so that it will not tip or fall off.

Once you have prepared the box and mixed the powder, you are ready to put in a flower. The flower either should be freshly picked or should have been kept fresh in a glass of water. First make sure there are no drops of water on the petals. Then cut off the stem.

If the stem is strong and stiff, you can save it, dry it on a piece of newspaper, and reattach it to the flower later. If you do not attach the dried flower to a stem you will need a stiff wire so that you can arrange it in a vase. If you plan to save the stem you have cut off, take off the leaves and side branches before you dry it.

If you are using silica gel, there should be no hole in the bottom of your box. Put two to three inches of silica gel in the box and stick the shortened flower stem into it. This will hold the blossom upright.

If you are using perlite or the cornmeal-borax mixture your box will have a hole in the bottom, and the stem should be stuck through it. Do not crush or bruise the petals while you are doing this. The stem should fit snugly into the hole. If the hole is too small, do not try to force the stem through it. Take the flower out of the box and make the hole a little bigger.

When the hole is big enough to admit the end of the stem, push the stem through just far enough so you can get hold of the end from the underside of the box. Pull down on the stem until the bottom of the flower is about one inch from the bottom of the box. Then place the box up on its props so that the stem hangs down into the space between them.

Now sprinkle some drying powder into the bottom of the box around the flower. You can use a teaspoon or your fingers to put the powder in the box. Push the powder under the flower with your fingers or use a small brush. You should have a layer of desiccant about a quarter of an inch deep under the petals. Then pull gently on the stem until the bottom petals just touch this layer of powder.

Now you are ready to cover the flower with powder. The method for doing this is the same no matter what kind of desiccant you are using. Sprinkle the desiccant on the flower a little at a time so that the powder sifts down among the petals. You can use your fingers or shake the powder from the tip of a teaspoon by tapping the teaspoon with your finger. Do not dump on the whole teaspoonful at once or the powder will flatten the petals and the flower will not look natural when it is dry.

Shaking the box a little or tapping it helps to sift the powder down between the petals. You may also find it helpful to push the desiccant around the flower with a small watercolor brush, but be careful not to crush or bend the petals. You do not have to fill the box with powder but the flower should be completely covered.

When the blossom is completely buried put the box in a safe place. Seal the box if you are using silica gel. Otherwise leave the box open.

It will take two or three weeks for the flower to dry, depending on the weather and the variety of flower. Flowers with a single row of petals, such as hollyhocks, will dry in about a week if the weather is dry. Flowers with many layers of petals, such as marigolds and zinnias, may take three weeks to dry.

You can usually tell whether the flower is dry by feeling the stem. If it is hard and brittle, the flower is probably ready to take out of the box. First test it by very gently brushing the desiccant off the top of the flower. If the petals feel crisp, the flower is dry enough to take out of the box. If the petals still feel soft, sprinkle the powder over them again and let the flower dry a few days longer.

Do not try to take it out until it is completely dry, or it will spoil.

When you are sure the flower is dry, pour the desiccant out of the box onto a piece of newspaper. Do this slowly. When the flower is completely exposed lift it carefully out of the box. Hold it upside down by the stem and shake the powder from between the petals. You can also brush them gently with a soft watercolor brush and blow on them. Do this very gently so as not to damage the petals.

When you have practiced burying a flower, you can dry more than one in the same box. Always bury flowers of the same type in a box so that they all dry in the same length of time. Use a box that is long enough and wide enough for the flowers to be buried without touching each other. If you use a cardboard box propped up on books, the box must be quite stiff and strong so that it will not sag or buckle when it is full of drying powder. Make the holes far enough apart to allow for plenty of room between each blossom.

You can also experiment with drying other types of flowers. Flat blossoms such as daisies are best dried upside down. In this case you will not need holes in the box. Make a low mound of desiccant on the bottom of the box and put the flower upside down on top of this mound,

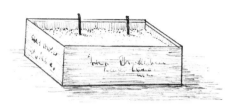

with the stem sticking up in the air. The underside of the flower should be covered, but it is not necessary to cover the stem with desiccant.

Most flower heads made up of many separate blossoms, such as geraniums, can be dried right-side-up, but some flower heads that are rather flat on the top, such as Queen Anne's lace and verbena, are best dried upside down.

Cup-shaped flowers, such as poppies and hollyhocks, should also be dried upside down. Fill the cup lightly with a fluffy piece of cotton before you turn the flower upside down. Then cover the back with drying powder. The cotton will help to keep the cup from being flattened.

If you want to try drying bell-shaped flowers, such as bluebells, and tube- or trumpet-shaped flowers, such as single petunias, place them right-side-up in the box and pile plenty of drying powder around the outside of the blossoms to support the petals before you put powder into the bell, tube, or trumpet.

A few flowers, such as individual hollyhock blossoms, have no stems at all, or such short stems that they should be given artificial stems of wire before they are dried.

114

Flowers with very thin, weak stems should also be given wire stems before they are dried. Use very thin wire for this purpose. You can usually get thin wire at florist shops or in the hardware store.

If the flower has a thickened base just below the petals, stick the wire through this base from side to side. Then bend the two ends down and twist them tightly together beneath the flower. You will need about six inches of wire to make a three-inch stem.

If the flower you plan to dry does not have a thickened base, push the wire down through the center of the flower. Bend one end of the wire into a short hook and push the straight end down through the flower until it comes out at the bottom. Then pull it down the rest of the way until the hook sinks into the top of the flower. You will only need about three inches of wire for this kind of artificial stem.

If you have trouble pushing the wire into either the top of the flower or the side of the thickened base without bending it, make a hole for the wire with a needle or long pin. As the flower dries it will shrink tightly around the wire.

Long spikes of flowers, such as delphinium, snapdragons, and stock, are best dried by placing them length-

115

wise in a long box. If you are going to bury them in silica gel, the whole blossom head and its stem must fit inside the airtight container. Otherwise you can leave a long stem on the spike of flowers, since you will be able to let the stem extend out through the side of the box.

A shoe box is long enough to hold most flower spikes. A few kinds of flowers, with very long spikes, may have to be put in one of the long narrow boxes that florists use.

Unless you are using silica gel to dry your flower spike, cut a slot for the stem in one end of the box. Its lower edge should be about one inch above the bottom. You can usually cut such a slot with a strong pair of scissors. If the cardboard is thick you may have to saw the slot with a bread knife. It will not be necessary to prop up the box on books or blocks, so it does not have to be made of such stiff cardboard as a box with holes in the bottom.

However, inside the box, it is best to support the flower spike; otherwise the flowers on the underside will be pressed flat against the box by the weight of the powder. The supports should raise the spike high enough to keep the flowers from touching the bottom of the box. Make

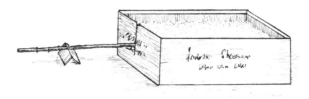

the supports out of squares of thin cardboard bent in half. A piece of cardboard about four inches square will hold the spike about an inch and a half above the bottom of the box.

The easiest way to bend a square of cardboard neatly in half is to make a pencil line across the center, using a ruler. Then place the square on a magazine or on a soft pad made of several thicknesses of newspaper. Place the edge of the ruler along the line you drew and trace over it again, pressing hard with the point of the pencil to dent the cardboard. You should use a rather blunt pencil so that the point will not break.

The dent you have made will help you to bend the cardboard in a straight line. Press the crease in the folded cardboard by laying it on a table and firmly rubbing the edge of your ruler over it. When you partly open the creased square of cardboard it will be shaped like a steep roof.

You will need enough of these supports to place them about four or five inches apart under the spike of flowers. If your plant has a long stem sticking out through the

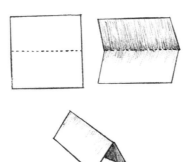

end of the box, you may also need one or two supports under this stem to keep it from drooping as it dries. If the stem is fairly thick and strong, it may not need supporting.

Before you place your spike in the box, sprinkle a layer of desiccant about half an inch deep on the bottom. Place the flower spike on top of this layer. The stem can be slipped down into the slot you made in the end of the box. It does not have to go all the way to the bottom of the slot—just far enough so the flowers on the underside barely touch the layer of desiccant. Adjust the supports under the flower spike. Try to place them so that the peak of the creased cardboard is against the stem, not the flowers.

You may now cover the spike with drying powder in the same way already described for burying other flowers.

In addition to drying full-blown flowers, dry some buds and partly opened flowers to scatter through your arrangements.

If you need to add extra stems to your dried flowers so they will be long enough to arrange in a vase, you may use either stiff, dry flower stalks; long, straight, slender, dry twigs from a shrub or tree; or pieces of fairly stiff wire. Goldenrod stalks and the stalks of tall phlox make strong stems. Wire stems are good because you can bend them into curves if you need to. You may use either galvanized wire that you buy in the hardware store or medium-weight florist's wire bought from a flower shop. You can sometimes use the wire of unpainted coat hangers, but you will find this a little too stiff and thick for many flowers. Wire stems should be stiff enough to hold flowers upright but flexible enough to be bent easily with the fingers.

Whether you use wire or natural stems, the artificial stalk should be about the same thickness as the original stalk you cut off. If you use natural stalks they should be dry. Cut off any side twigs. Stems about a foot long are long enough to use in most flower arrangements, but you should make them longer if you plan to put your arrangement in a big vase.

You can fasten the short flower stem to its artificial stalk by wrapping them together with floral tape. This is a stretchy green tape that clings to itself but is not gluey. It can be bought in most flower shops and in some garden-supply stores and hardware stores.

Place the tip of the artificial stem right up against the base of the flower. Hold the short flower stalk tightly against the top of the stem you are adding. Start by wind-

ing the tape right under the flower. Then wind it down around the two stems in overlapping spirals. It is usually best to cover the whole length of the added stem with tape so that it will not look patched. You can make a spike of several flowers by adding single flowers down the stem one under the other after every few spirals of tape.

If you cannot get floral tape, you can glue your flower to the end of the long stem. The transparent cement used for mending china is good for this purpose because it will stick to wire as well as to a natural stem.

In order to glue the natural stem to the artificial stem these must be laid side by side on a flat surface covered with waxed paper. Waxed paper will not stick tightly to dry glue, so you will be able to peel it off glued stems. Put the waxed paper on top of a big thick book and lay your flower on top, with the stem on the book but the head hanging over the edge. You may have to slip something under the blossom to raise it a little so that its stem will lie flat on the waxed paper and it will not tip off the book. Magazines are useful for propping up the flower head. You can put as many pages under the flower as necessary.

Smear some glue on the top three inches of the dried stalk or wire you are going to fasten to the flower stem.

120

Lay this glued stem on the waxed paper against the short stem of your flower. The tip of the long stem should touch the bottom of the flower and the two stems should be tight against each other.

If your book is big enough and you have properly propped up the flower, the two stems will stay in place against each other until the glue has hardened. If for some reason the two stems do not stay together, put another piece of waxed paper over the glued joint and put a small object on top of this piece of paper to hold the two ends together.

Glue covered by waxed paper hardens very slowly because it gets no air. If you have put a piece of waxed paper over the gluey stems, you should take it off after about fifteen minutes. Be very careful not to move the stems as you peel off the paper. The glue will still be quite soft. Let the glue on the top of the joint harden for about ten minutes. Then slide the joined stems sideways and roll them over so the underside can get air.

If you have not had to weigh down the joint, the glue on the top and sides of the joined stems will harden in about ten minutes and you can carefully turn the stems

Boxwood

over so that the glue on the underside can get hard. Let the glue harden for two or three hours before you pick up the flower. Once the glue is thoroughly hard, your dried flower will be firmly fastened to its new stem and you can put it in an arrangement.

You may want to dry a few leafy branches to use as a background in your flower arrangement. It is best to choose branches with rather small leaves. Boxwood, laurel, beech, the many species of *Spiraea,* and box-leaved holly (*Ilex crenata convexa*) dry well and will stay fairly green if they are not exposed to bright sunlight. The trailing stems of the evergreen ground cover *Vinca minor,* which is commonly called either myrtle or periwinkle, dry well and are a graceful addition to an arrangement.

The silvery gray leaves of Russian olive (*Elaeagnus angustifolia*) and the woolly white leaves of dusty miller (*Artemisia stelleriana*), which grows on sandy dunes and beaches, dry beautifully and are lovely in flower arrangements.

Colored autumn leaves will keep their brilliant color when dried in desiccants. These frequently are not firmly attached to the twigs, however, since they are about to fall off the tree anyway. If you plan to dry a branch of autumn leaves, cut it just as soon as the leaves are colored and before there has been a frost. It is also a good idea

Russian olive

Periwinkle

to put a tiny drop of transparent glue or cement where the end of each leaf stem is attached to the twig. Let the glue dry thoroughly before you bury the branch in a desiccant.

You will need a very big box to hold your branch without bending it. Perlite is a good desiccant to use for drying leafy branches.

SPRAYING DRIED PLANTS

Any of the seed heads, seed capsules, leaves, and flowers that you have dried either in the air or by burying them in desiccants may be sprayed with liquid plastic. This gives them a glossy appearance and helps to keep the colors from fading.

There is no need to spray material that has been air-dried. Most of the sturdier seed heads and flowers will last for a long time without being sprayed. Dried bouquets that are as much as fifteen years old can look almost as good as new, although their colors will not be as bright as when they were first picked.

Flowers that have to be dried in desiccants are likely to be more fragile than most air-dried plants because they have large, thin petals. Spraying these with liquid plastic will not only keep their colors brighter but will make the plants less likely to break. It will also keep them from absorbing moisture out of the air, which would make them limp.

To spray dried flowers and leaves, stand the stalks one at a time in a milk carton or jar filled with sand to hold the stalk steady. Hang some newspaper behind the plant and put newspaper under the jar to protect the wall and furniture. You can fasten newspaper to a painted wall by sticking it on with two or three pieces of masking tape.

This tape will peel off a painted surface without leaving a mark. Do not use it on wallpaper, however.

Hold the spray can about one foot away from the plant. Be sure you are aiming away from your face. Do not spray too much on the plant at one time. Several light coatings are better than one heavy coat. If you get delicate petals too wet they may collapse. After each squirt of spray turn the jar so that you coat the plant evenly on all sides. Let each coat dry thoroughly before you put on the next. And let the plant dry thoroughly before taking it out of the jar.

PRESERVING LEAVES WITH LIQUID PRESERVATIVE

It is possible to preserve the leaves of many plants without drying them. Leaves that are preserved with a liquid preservative do not become stiff and brittle. They retain their natural texture and pliability and are consequently less breakable than dried leaves. They usually do not keep their natural color, however. Thin leaves tend to turn olive green. Thicker leaves are likely to become tan or brown. These can be very handsome in arrangements. The maroon leaves of red-leaved barberry, cherry, and beech usu-

American beech

American holly

ally stay their natural dark red color. Most colored autumn leaves cannot be preserved in this way because autumn leaves are no longer able to suck up liquid after they have changed color.

Curing foliage in liquid preservative depends on the power that leaves have to suck up moisture through the cut end of the branch to which they are attached. Most leaves can be preserved by this method as long as they are fully grown but not old. Leaves that do not wilt after they have been cut and left out of water for an hour or two are usually suitable for preserving.

The preservative that is used is glycerin—a rather thick, transparent liquid. You can buy glycerin at the drugstore. It must be mixed with water to make it thin enough for the plant to suck up. The amount of glycerin and water that you mix together depends on the texture of the leaves you plan to preserve.

For preserving thick-textured leaves, such as those of rhododendron and evergreen magnolia, mix one cup of glycerin with two cups of water. For medium-thick leaves, such as camellia, beech, holly, and ivy, mix one cup of glycerin with two and a half cups of water. For thin leaves use one cup of glycerin mixed with three cups of water.

Cut off the end of the stem of the plant you are

126

planning to preserve just before you put it in the preserving fluid. The ends of woody branches should be mashed and splintered by hitting them with a hammer.

Mix a batch of preserving fluid and pour enough into a transparent glass jar or bottle to cover about three or four inches of the cut end of the stem. Stand your spray of leaves in this mixture so they can suck it up. If you put the jar in the bright sun the leaves will become bleached. Leaves that are preserved and kept in a dark corner stay greener and darker.

Ivy should be completely covered with preserving fluid, leaves and all, for about four days. Then it should be taken out and rinsed in cold water before it is put in an arrangement.

Not all leaves can be preserved as quickly. Most thin-textured leaves will take about a week. They should not be taken out of the preserving fluid until they turn olive green. Medium-thick leaves usually turn brownish when they are preserved. This may take three or four weeks. Thick leaves also turn brown and may take as long as eight weeks before they are thoroughly preserved.

Until the leaves change color, the stem end must be kept covered with preserving fluid. Mark the level of the liquid in your jar with a felt pen or china marking pencil.

English ivy

127

Keep the fluid at this level as long as the stem is still sucking. Add more fluid when necessary.

The leaves should stay soft and pliable while they are standing in the preserving fluid. They should not wilt. If they start to wilt it means they are not sucking properly. Take out the stem and recut the end. Mash it again if it is woody. Then put the stem back in the jar and add a little water to the preserving fluid to make it thinner.

Once the leaves are thoroughly preserved they will stay soft and pliable without wilting even when they are not in liquid.

You can save the preserving fluid for reuse by straining it through a thin piece of cloth and keeping it in a covered jar or bottle.

Highbush cranberry

8
ARRANGEMENTS OF PRESERVED PLANTS

Arranging plants that have been dried in desiccants or in the air, or preserved with glycerin water, is not very different from arranging fresh flowers except that you should not put them in water.

You can arrange your plant material in an empty vase if you wish. But you will find it easier to place each stem exactly in the position you want it if you put something in the container to hold the stems in place.

If you are going to arrange your plants in a deep vase or bowl, dry sand or small pebbles are excellent for holding the stems in place. If you do not live where you can easily get sand or pebbles, you can use the kind of fine grit sold in pet stores for fishbowls. Or you can use the gravelly mixture sold in bags to put in cats' litter boxes.

Arrangements of Preserved Plants

Fill your container almost to the rim with sand or pebbles. You should have a layer at least three inches deep into which you stick the ends of the stems. Push the dried stems gently but firmly into place. Thin, brittle stalks break easily. It is best to hold them near the bottom as you insert them into the sand.

If you want to make your arrangement in a flat dish that will not hold a deep enough layer of sand, you can stick the stems into a lump of plasticine instead. Plasticine is the waxy kind of modeling clay that never gets completely hard.

The lump of plasticine should be at least two inches thick. Soften it well by kneading it with your hands and roll it into a ball. Press this soft ball firmly to the bottom of the container. Stick the ends of the plant stems into this mound. You can use a toothpick or pencil to make holes in the lump of plasticine if the stems of your flowers are weak and brittle. Press the plasticine around each stem end once you have it correctly placed so that it will stay in the position you want it. You will find it easier to do this if you do not have too many stems in your arrangement.

You can put as many stems in sand as you can fit into the vase. But it is quite possible to make very attractive

arrangements of only a few carefully chosen stems. Try placing two or three dried flowers near the bottom of a single branch of colorful autumn leaves. This can be as lovely as a vase full of many flowers and leaves. If you arrange your stems in a flat dish you can arrange them in one group of several stems or you can stick two or three lumps of plasticine to the bottom of the dish and insert just a few stems into each lump. Your arrangement will be more interesting if the groups are not all the same size.

You should decide where you are going to place your arrangement before you make it. If it is going to be flat against a wall, you should arrange the plants so that the side next to the wall will be flat. This is particularly true if you are planning to fill your vase very full of plants. You do not have to worry how the side against the wall looks because nobody can see it.

You will find it easier to make this kind of arrangement if you first place the tallest stalks in the back of the vase. These will make a background against which you can next place stems of medium height. Put short flowers in the front part of your arrangement last of all.

131

Arrangements that are going to be placed in a prominent position on a table should usually be lower than arrangements that are against a wall. They should also be made to look well from every side. To make this kind of arrangement, first place your taller stalks in the center of the container. Then work toward the rim. Turn the vase as you put in the stalks so that you can see how it looks from every angle.

An arrangement that is to be placed on a dining-room table should always be low enough so that people can see each other over it.

Take plenty of time to put your plants in position, since an arrangement of preserved plants will last for several months.

132

CLEANING PRESERVED PLANTS

After a few months in a vase your preserved plants will get quite dusty. By then you may be tired of them anyway and, if it is spring, you may want to replace them with fresh flowers.

It is quite possible, however, to clean and rearrange most preserved plants. Most air-dried flowers and seed heads, whether or not they have been sprayed with liquid plastic, can be washed without doing them any harm. Leafy branches that have been preserved with glycerin water can usually be washed also. Most flowers that have been dried in desiccants cannot be washed unless the blossoms and most of the upper stem are thoroughly coated with liquid plastic. Even such plastic-coated flowers are often too fragile to be cleaned without damage and have to be thrown away when they become dusty and dingy.

You should always handle any preserved plant carefully. Pull the stalks one at a time out of the container in which they are arranged. Swish each stalk gently up and down and back and forth several times in a basinful of lukewarm water. You will have to change the water quite often, since it will get very dirty.

133

Spread the wet stalks out on several thicknesses of newspaper and let them dry thoroughly before rearranging them.

Arranging flowers, whether they are fresh or preserved, so that they look really well is an art that requires a great deal of practice. The more you do it, the more expert you will become. You will also discover which combinations of plants look particularly attractive together and which plants look best in certain vases and in certain rooms.

No two flower arrangements and no two flower pictures ever look exactly alike. This is part of the fun. Every time you arrange flowers in a vase or on a paper background you are experimenting. And each time you will create something new and special.

Though it takes time and patience to dry flowers and arrange them into a picture or in a container, it is very satisfying to be creating something beautiful that you will be able to enjoy for a long time.

A LIST OF
FIELD GUIDES

These books will help you identify the plants you find. They picture and describe wild flowers, ferns, shrubs, and trees that grow in various parts of the United States and give their common and botanical names. All these books have black-and-white drawings or photographs of the plants, and some also have colored pictures. You should be able to find these books in the public library. They can also be bought at your bookstore or obtained by writing to the publisher.

In addition, there are books available in the national parks. Almost every national park has on sale paperbound books showing the plants you will see in that particular park. These are often very helpful in identifying plants that grow near the park as well as inside it. Also, your public library probably has other books about the wild plants in the area in which you live.

Beginner's Guide to Wild Flowers, by Ethel H. Housman. New York: G. P. Putnam's Sons, 1955.

California Desert Wildflowers, by Philip A. Munz. Berkeley, California: University of California Press, 1962. Paperbound edition available.

California Mountain Wildflowers, by Philip A. Munz. Berkeley, California: University of California Press, 1963. Paperbound edition available.

California Spring Wildflowers, by Philip A. Munz. Berkeley, California: University of California Press, 1961. Paperbound edition available.

Common Plants of the Southern California Mountains, by Harold F. De Lisle. Healdsburg, California: Naturegraph Publishers, 1961. Paperbound edition available.

Desert Wild Flowers, by Edmund Jaeger. Stanford, California: Stanford University Press, revised 1968. Paperbound edition available.

136

A List of Field Guides

The Doubleday First Guide to Wild Flowers, by Millicent Selsam. New York: Doubleday and Company, Inc., 1964.

Ferns of the Northwest, by Theodore C. Frye. Portland, Oregon: Binfords and Mort, Publishers, 1934.

Field Book of American Wild Flowers, by F. Schuyler Mathews. New York: G. P. Putnam's Sons, 1955.

Field Book of Western Wild Flowers, by Margaret Armstrong. New York: G. P. Putnam's Sons, 1915.

A Field Guide to the Ferns and Their Related Families of Northeast and Central North America, by Boughton Cobb. Boston: Houghton Mifflin Company, 1956.

A Field Guide to Rocky Mountain Wildflowers from Northern Arizona and New Mexico to British Columbia, by John J. Craighead, Frank C. Craighead, Jr., and Ray J. Davis. Boston: Houghton Mifflin Company, 1963.

A Field Guide to the Trees and Shrubs of Northeastern and North-Central United States and South-Central Canada, by George A. Petrides. Boston: Houghton Mifflin Company, 1958.

A Field Guide to Wildflowers of Northeastern and North-Central North America, by Roger T. Peterson. Boston: Houghton Mifflin Company, 1968.

137

A List of Field Guides

The First Book of Wild Flowers, by Betty Cavanna. New York: Franklin Watts, Inc., 1961.

Flowers: A Guide to Familiar American Wild Flowers, by Herbert S. Zim and Alexander C. Martin. New York: Golden Press, 1950. Paperbound edition available.

Flowers of the Southwest Desert, by Natt N. Dodge. Globe, Arizona: Southwest Monuments Association, 1965.

Great Smoky Mountain Wildflowers, by Carlos Campbell *et al.* Chattanooga, Tennessee: University of Tennessee Press, 1964. Paperbound.

How to Know the Western Trees, by Harry Baerg. Dubuque, Iowa: W. C. Brown, 1955. Paperbound edition available.

The Macmillan Wild Flower Book, by Clarence J. Hylander. New York: The Macmillan Company, 1954.

Michigan Wildflowers, by Helen V. Smith. Bloomfield Hills, Michigan: Cranbrook Institute of Science, 1966.

The New Field Book of American Wild Flowers, by Harold W. Rickett. New York: G. P. Putnam's Sons, 1963.

Recognizing Flowering Wild Plants, by William C. Grimm. Harrisburg, Pennsylvania: Stackpole Books, 1968.

Redwood Empire Wildflower Jewels, by Dorothy Young. Healdsburg, California: Naturegraph Publishers, 1964. Paperbound edition available.

Roadside Flowers of Texas, by Mary M. Wills. Austin, Texas: University of Texas Press, 1961.

Roadside Wildflowers in Southwest Uplands, by Natt N. Dodge. Globe, Arizona: Southwest Monuments Association, 1967. Paperbound.

Shore Wildflowers of California, Oregon, and Washington, by Philip A. Munz. Berkeley, California: University of California Press, 1965.

The Shrub Identification Book: The Visual Method for the Practical Identification of Shrubs, Including Woody Vines and Ground Covers, by George W. D. Symonds. New York: M. Barrows and Company, 1963.

The Tree Identification Book: A New Method for the Practical Identification and Recognition of Trees, by George W. D. Symonds. New York: M. Barrows and Company, 1958.

Wild Flowers, by Homer D. House. New York: The Macmillan Company, 1961.

The Wild Flowers of California, by Mary E. Parsons. New York: Dover Publications, Inc., 1966. Paperbound reprint of 1907 edition.

139

A List of Field Guides

Wildflowers of Cape Cod, by Harold and Hathaway W. Hinds. Chatham, Massachusetts: Chatham Press, 1968.

Wild Flowers of North America in Full Color, by Robert S. Lemmon and Charles C. Johnson. New York: Doubleday and Company, Inc., 1961.

Wild Flowers of North Carolina, by William S. Justice and C. R. Bell. Chapel Hill, North Carolina: University of North Carolina Press, 1968.

Wild Flowers of the Pacific Coast, by Leslie L. Haskin. Portland, Oregon: Binfords and Mort, Publishers, 1934.

Wild Flowers in South Carolina, by Wade D. Batson. Columbia, South Carolina: University of South Carolina Press, 1964.

Wild Flowers of Washington State, by Ellis H. Robinson. Lynwood, Washington: Ellis H. Robinson, 1964. Paperbound.

WHERE TO SEND FOR SEED CATALOGS

Breck's of Boston, 200 Breck Bldg., Boston, Mass.,
02210

Burgess Seed and Plant Co., Galesburg, Mich., 49053

W. Atlee Burpee Co., Philadelphia, Pa., 19132

Gurney Seed and Nursery Co., Yankton, S. Dak.,
57078

Joseph Harris Co., Inc., Rochester, N.Y., 14611

George W. Park Seed Co., Greenwood, S.C., 29646

Vaughan's Seed Co., 24 Vesey St., New York, N.Y.,
10024

INDEX

Page numbers in boldface indicate illustrations. Botanical names are in italics. Only the generic name is given after the common name (e.g., astilbe, *Astilbe*) when several species of the same genus are very similar and can all be used for the same purpose. When plants of several genera all have the same common name (e.g., heather) and can all be used for the same purpose, several generic names may be listed after the common name. When a specific plant is illustrated or mentioned in the text, both the generic name and the specific name are given after the common name (e.g., Queen's Lace, *Daucus carota*).

Index

Index

Index

Index

Index

Index

Index

sunrays, *see* acroclinium

supports for flower spikes, 116–118

tansy, *Tanacetum vulgare*, **99–100**

tape:
  floral, 118–120
  sticky, 57–58

teasel, *Dipsacus sylvestris*, 96, **97**

thistle, *Cirsium* (*see also* globe thistle), 96
  bull, *Cirsium vulgare*, **97**

thorn, *see* fire thorn

thrift, sea, *Armeria*, **104**

traveler's joy, *see* virgin's bower

trays, decorated, 85

verbena, *Abronia, Verbena*, 114

vetch, cow, *Vicia cracca*, **7**

vinyl, *see* plastic

violets, *Viola*, 12–13
  bird's-foot, *Viola pedata*, **49**

virgin's bower, *Clematis virginiana*, 90–**91**

wahoo, *see* burning bush

waxwork, *see* bittersweet

wheat, *Triticum, see* grasses

willow, pussy, *Salix discolor*, 95–**96**

winecups, *Callirhoe involucrata*, **10**

wreaths, as picture designs, 47–48, **51**, 81

yarrow, *Achillea*, 98
  common, *Achillea millefolium*, **98**

yucca, *Yucca filamentosa*, 92, **94**

zinnias, *Zinnia*, 33–34, 105, 112

ABOUT THE AUTHOR

Laura Louise Foster has been interested in everything in the natural world since she was a small child. She was a collector, and remembers her bedroom as "a combination museum and zoo, and a terrible mess." Pressing flowers was an early childhood pastime, and in her teens she dried flowers for pictures and arrangements.

Mrs. Foster has taught nature study and has written and illustrated numerous botanical articles. She is now a professional landscape designer with her husband, and she grows and draws flowers and other plant material. Her drawings of ferns are in the Hunt Botanical Library of the Carnegie Institute in Pittsburgh.